Project Communications

Project Communications

A Critical Factor for Project Success

Connie Plowman, PMP
Jill Diffendal

BEP BUSINESS EXPERT PRESS

Project Communications: A Critical Factor for Project Success
Copyright © Business Expert Press, LLC, 2020.

First published in 2020 by
Business Expert Press, LLC
222 East 46th Street, New York, NY 10017
www.businessexpertpress.com

ISBN-13: 978-1-95152-772-3 (paperback)
ISBN-13: 978-1-95152-773-0 (e-book)

Business Expert Press Portfolio and Project Management Collection

Collection ISSN: 2156-8189 (print)
Collection ISSN: 2156-8200 (electronic)

Cover design by Aaron Roshong and interior design by S4Carlisle Publishing Services Private Ltd., Chennai, India

First edition: 2020

10 9 8 7 6 5 4 3 2 1

Disclaimer

Abstract

Communication is vital for project success. Experts know it. Industry-wide research verifies it. Yet projects continue to fail because of poor communication. As a result, stakeholders and organizations don't realize the benefits of their projects and project teams.

This book presents a new way to look at communication within projects. It combines real-world examples and practical tips with theory, research, and professional standards you can apply to any size and type of project. Gain actionable insights into identifying your audience, choosing the right tools, managing change, and handling conflict. Expand your professional toolkit with templates, activities, and resources. Develop your project communications expertise with reflective questions and recommendations.

Whether you are a project manager, team member, project sponsor, or stakeholder, this book is for you. For educators, the book is ideal for students studying project management and related fields.

Make *your* project communications a critical factor in *your* project success!

Keywords

agile project teams; communication; project communication; project communications management plan; project communication tools; project risk; stakeholders; traditional project teams; uncertainty management theory; uncertainty reduction theory; virtual project teams

Contents

Preface

Meet Connie Plowman. Throughout her career she has traveled the road of project management—as a project manager, sponsor, team member, and in many other project roles.

Meet Jill Diffendal. Throughout her career she has traveled the road of communication—as a writer, editor, content contributor, and in many other communication roles.

Then our two roads met, and a project was launched to write a book about project communications. We were first connected by an introductory email from a mutual colleague—one of many different forms of communication that took place on this project. As we wrote this book, we found ourselves using, practicing, and experimenting with the same project communication practices that you will read about in these pages.

Like many project teams starting out, there was uncertainty, both about the project and with each other. We eliminated uncertainty by developing, and using, a project communications management plan. We made changes when the plan needed adjustment. We set clear expectations, listened to each other's ideas, provided feedback, communicated with stakeholders, used many different tools and techniques to effectively communicate—including our talents and strengths—and ultimately, built trust.

We do not present this book as the "be all, end all" in project communications. Rather, it is a resource to encourage you to broaden the way you look at communicating on projects, and to offer insights, tools, and techniques to bring that perspective into your projects.

Effective communication leads to project success. We know it. We experienced it. We completed the book on time, within scope, and under budget.

When it comes to project communications, we walk the talk. So can you!

Acknowledgments

To our terrific editor, Tim Kloppenborg, special thanks for bringing us together and encouraging us to put our project communications thoughts and experiences on paper. Thank you, Tim, for your ongoing support, guidance, and confidence in bringing this book to life.

To our awesome peer reviewers, Debbie Austin, Martha Buelt, Diane Cooney, Sara Webber, and Shannon Heizenrader, we can't thank you enough for giving us your precious time and valuable input.

To our amazing graphic designer, Aaron Roshong, thank you for lending us your exceptional talent in creating the graphics for this book and making it even better.

To our great colleagues, students, clients, and customers, sincere thanks for a lifetime of learning in how effective communications can truly make a difference in projects—and in life.

And finally, to our wonderful family and friends—we couldn't have done this without you!

CHAPTER 1

Introduction

As long as there is communication, everything can be solved.[1]
—Robert Trujillo, bassist for the rock band Metallica

Think about any time you have needed to work with another person to accomplish something. Did you coordinate with your spouse this morning to determine who would pack your children's lunches or pick them up after soccer practice? Did you call the doctor's office to schedule an appointment? Did you send or respond to a meeting invitation at work? Did you speak with your boss about a project assignment or to prioritize your workload?

Communication is *how* people work together to get things done. Without it, the kids would never get picked up from school (or get there in the first place). You would never see the doctor (or tell him what ails you). You would never meet with your colleagues (or discuss the tasks at hand with them). You would never understand your project assignment (or receive it in the first place).

Still not convinced? Try spending an hour at work without communicating. Do not read or respond to any e-mails, use the phone, attend a meeting, speak to coworkers. You're probably thinking, "That's impossible!"

Exactly.

In a project, communication is vital because the project is a new endeavor for every stakeholder involved. Even if every member of the team has worked together on dozens of projects before this one, every project is unique. Communication is how stakeholders understand what this project is about, how it will affect them, and what role they may be expected to play.

There are a number of resources available on communication in project management. Most of those resources, however, focus on the "how"—the tools and techniques project managers, project teams, and stakeholders can use. This book will take a step back to look at communication more holistically as *the* way projects—and just about everything else that involves more than one person—get done. So let's get started. Welcome to Chapter 1.

The purpose of this chapter is to help you:

- Understand why project communication is so important
- Know what to expect from this book: what it will cover, who the audience is, how the book is structured, and key definitions
- Trace the evolution of project communications

Are you ready? We are!

Why Is Communication So Important in Projects?

Communication is, of course, a necessity in projects. But just how important is it? Good communication skills separate good project managers from the rest of the pack, and separate successful projects from unsuccessful ones. Research from the Project Management Institute (PMI) and other sources shows that project communication has a significant impact on project budgets and project success. In 2013, PMI published an in-depth report on "The Essential Role of Communications" in project management, with conclusions derived from the organization's annual, global *Pulse of the Profession®* survey. This report revealed how impactful project communications are.

- Effective communication to all stakeholders is "the most crucial success factor in project management."
- 7.5 percent of every dollar spent on a project is at risk due to ineffective communication.
- Effective communication leads to a 17-percent increase in finishing projects within budget.
- Half of all unsuccessful projects fall short due to ineffective communication.

- High-performing organizations create project communications management plans for nearly twice as many projects as low-performing organizations (see more about project communications management plans in Chapter 5).
- High-performing organizations also perform significantly better at delivering the message in a timely manner, with sufficient detail and clarity, using nontechnical language, through appropriate communication channels/media.[2]

In another study of 448 innovative projects, researchers found that interpersonal skills including communication were more predictive of project success than traditional project management skills such as planning and controlling activities. These interpersonal skills are what separate leaders from managers, and become more important to project success as the complexity and innovativeness of the project increases.[3]

With so much evidence demonstrating the value that effective communication can bring to a project, why do project communications continue to fall short, thereby putting projects at risk? The literature reveals at least two reasons.

First, project managers do not always follow or prioritize good communication practices. In one study of several projects at a large IT service provider, only a small percentage of the projects had a formal communications plan, and performance reports and lessons learned were not frequently utilized. This was despite the company having well-defined communication processes in its project management framework.[4]

Second, project managers may take a narrow, transactional view of communication as a means of delivering information about the project. In a study of communication practices of project managers at a large international bank, 82 percent viewed communication as a means to transmit clear and complete information about the project.[5]

Communication, however, is much more than simply sending and receiving information. It is a mechanism to reduce uncertainty, build trust, demonstrate leadership, generate support, manage change, mitigate conflict, and facilitate stakeholder satisfaction—all key elements to a project's success.

Which is why we wrote this book.

Communication is much more than simply sending and receiving information. It is a mechanism to reduce uncertainty, build trust, demonstrate leadership, generate support, manage change, mitigate conflict, and facilitate stakeholder satisfaction—all key elements to a project's success.

What to Expect from This Book

This book intends to help you apply theory and best practices from the communication world to enhance your understanding and execution of the communication aspects of project management. It may reconfirm some of the techniques and approaches you already use. We also hope that it helps you look at project communications more holistically, giving you some new ideas to try. The goal is not to achieve perfect communications in a project—that is unrealistic to define, much less accomplish. Rather, our purpose is to demonstrate the importance of good communication in any project, and to help you improve your project communications to have more successful projects, more satisfied stakeholders, and more productive project teams.

Remember that there is no "one-size-fits-all" approach to any aspect of project management, including project communication. Everything from the style and tone of your messages, to the tools and technology you use to create and deliver them, needs to be modified and adapted to suit the project (and the stakeholders) at hand. Some of what is presented in this book will make perfect sense in your current projects, while other information may not apply. Use what fits, and modify it as necessary to accomplish your communication and project goals. Most of all, enjoy the learning and practical experience, and keep track of lessons learned to help you communicate even more effectively in future projects.

Who This Book Is for

This book is designed for project managers, team members, project sponsors, and all stakeholders who are impacted by project actions, decisions, and outcomes. While the book directly addresses project managers, all other project stakeholders can learn from the information presented here to improve the way they communicate, both within projects and in many other contexts. In addition, educators can benefit by using this book in the classroom with students studying project management and project communication.

What You Will Find in This Book

We begin with an overview of the importance of project communication, and travel through time to reflect on the evolution of project communication. In Chapter 2, we will take a deeper look at communication theories that fit well within the project management context. These theories are based on the concept of uncertainty, how it affects people's attitudes and behaviors, and how you can use communication to minimize the impact of uncertainties on your project. Chapter 3 looks at the concept of audience, including how to identify the audience of your project, and how to tailor your communications to engage your audience in ways that will support the success of the project.

Chapter 4 reviews some of the "basics" and "things to consider" when communicating on projects, along with looking at why high-performing organizations and project teams are better at communicating. Chapters 5 and 6 cover the Project Communications Management Knowledge Area as outlined in *A Guide to the Project Management Body of Knowledge* (*PMBOK® Guide*), a widely used set of project management standards published by PMI. Chapter 5 covers planning project communications, while Chapter 6 reviews managing and monitoring project communications. Then in Chapter 7 we will review common tools used to communicate in projects. Note that this chapter does not highlight specific tools (e.g. Slack® or GoToMeeting™); rather, it provides considerations on various types of tools available, along with some guidelines on how to choose the right communication tool(s) for your project.

We'll conclude with two topics that share a significant overlap with communication within projects, and also apply more broadly within organizations. Chapter 8 looks at the process and nascent field of change management, emphasizing concepts that can help you communicate the changes your project will create for your stakeholders. In Chapter 9, we look at conflict management and share communication-based strategies for handling conflict within the project team, and with stakeholders outside the team. Chapter 10 concludes with a review of what you can take away from this book, both conceptually and practically, including how to build a personalized action plan to grow your project communication skills.

Each chapter begins with specific chapter objectives, uses examples that demonstrate the practical relevance of the information, and includes templates and other tools and activities you can use to apply the concepts in your current and future projects. Each chapter concludes with a summary of what was covered. There are also key questions to encourage reflection on the information, how it can be applied to your projects, and how it can be used in your own professional development. These key questions can also be useful in educational environments to stimulate students' critical thinking about applying these concepts to practice.

In Chapters 3 to 9, the end of each chapter also includes a special "Putting it into Practice" section that provides practical tips for applying the chapter's information in specific project contexts such as:

- traditional (also called "waterfall") project teams (colocated teams),
- agile project teams, and
- virtual project teams (also called distributed project teams; those that are not colocated and so have limited opportunity for face-to-face communication).

The book concludes with appendices that provide additional resources, templates, and other information for your use and reference.

Key Definitions

Before progressing further, let's take a moment to define some terms we will use often in this book. As we discuss further in Chapter 4, words matter, and using language that everyone understands is a critical aspect of clear and effective communication. So, let's provide some basic definitions to ensure a common understanding.

- **Agile project teams:** Agile project teams are those that work on projects using an agile or iterative approach. Rather than planning the full project at initiation, agile projects are planned in sprints of a set period of time (for example, 1 week or 2 months) that have a set list of goals/deliverables. Once the sprint is complete, the project is evaluated, and the next sprint is planned. This allows for changes and decisions to be made throughout the project as it progresses.

- **Communication:** There are three aspects of the term communication that we will explore in this book. First, it is a discipline within the social sciences that studies the way in which human beings share meaning through verbal, nonverbal, and symbolic (words and images) messages. Second, it is the act of transmitting and receiving those messages. Third, it is the tools or methods we use to transmit those messages.
- **Project communication:** This refers to the communication that takes place among project stakeholders and is related to some aspect of the project and its execution.
- **Project communications management plan:** This is a plan that outlines when, how, and what to communicate to various stakeholder groups throughout the duration of the project.
- **Project communication tools:** Project communication tools can be a wide range of technologies, documents, devices, interactions, and skills. For the purposes of this book, we define project communication tools as any mechanism or strategy to exchange information, reduce uncertainty, engage stakeholders, build trust, generate support for the project, and, ultimately, deliver project and team success.
- **Project risk:** A risk is an event or condition that may occur, resulting in a positive and/or negative effect on the project.
- **Stakeholders:** Stakeholders are anyone who affects or is affected by the project. This includes the project team, leadership who have authority over the project (such as the project sponsor), and others both inside and outside the organization who could be affected by the activities or outcomes of the project. At times we will distinguish different groups of stakeholders, since communication needs and approaches can differ based on the stakeholders' relationship to the project.
- **Traditional project teams:** Traditional project teams are those that use a traditional (or "waterfall") methodology. This is a linear

approach where most of the planning for the entire project is done after the initiation of the project.

- **Uncertainty management theory:** This is a theory in the field of communication that proposes that uncertainty is both a cognitive (knowledge-based) and emotional state. People may or may not communicate to reduce uncertainty.

- **Uncertainty reduction theory:** This is a theory in the field of communication that proposes that uncertainty is a cognitive state based on an individual's knowledge, and is separate from emotion. People will communicate in order to reduce uncertainty.

- **Virtual project teams:** Virtual (or distributed) project teams are those that involve individuals who are not geographically colocated. These teams generally rely heavily on technology to maintain communication, as face-to-face interactions are limited or nonexistent.

Now that we have covered these key concepts, let's take a quick trip through history to look at how project communication has evolved over time, through the lens of the *PMBOK® Guide*. Why look back? The *PMBOK® Guide* is written by project management professionals from around the world. A review will show how project communication (and project management knowledge) has changed and progressed as the profession itself has grown and matured. This may also give you a greater appreciation for how *your* project communication and approaches have developed, and can continue to evolve, over time.

The Evolution of Communications in the PMBOK® Guide

As project management has progressed since it first emerged as a profession in the middle of the last century, so has the approach to project communication. Understanding this historical context is a great place to start our conversation on project communication. So let's look at how the subject has changed in one of the seminal sources of information about project management practice, *A Guide to the Project Management Body of Knowledge*, or *PMBOK® Guide*, published by PMI and currently in its sixth edition. Figure 1.1 provides a high-level overview of this evolution, while the rest of this section traces the progression in more detail.

PMBOK® Guide 1st edition (1996)	• Communications is for information dissemination • Differentiation between general communications skills and communications in project management • Expectation for stakeholders to understand project language • Project Communications Management Knowledge Area is 8 pages, includes 4 processes
PMBOK® Guide 2nd edition (2000)	• Relatively few changes • Expectation for stakeholders to understand project language is no longer included • Knowledge Area is 10 pages, same 4 processes as first edition
PMBOK® Guide 3rd edition (2004)	• View of communication begins to broaden, with an emphasis on the importance of meeting the communications needs of stakeholders • Introduces basic communications model of sender-message-receiver • Administrative Closure process removed, Manage Stakeholders process added • Knowledge Area is 16 pages; 4 processes (with changes as noted above)
PMBOK® Guide 4th edition (2008)	• Clearly states that project managers spend the majority of their time communicating • Identify Stakeholders process added • Increasing emphasis on stakeholders as partners in ensuring project success • Knowledge Area jumps to 29 pages, 5 processes
PMBOK® Guide 5th edition (2013)	• Stakeholder Management separated into its own Knowledge Area • Knowledge Area decreases to 22 pages, 3 processes: Plan Communications Management, Manage Communications, and Control Communications
PMBOK® Guide 6th edition (2017)	• Purpose of communications is ensuring the information needs of stakeholders are met • New concepts are added: Key Concepts, Trends and Emerging Practices, Tailoring Considerations, Considerations for Agile/Adaptive Environments • Knowledge Area jumps to 35 pages, 3 processes (same as 5th edition, with one change: Control Communications is renamed to Monitor Communications)

Figure 1.1 An overview of the evolution of the Project Communications Management Knowledge Area in the PMBOK® Guide

First Edition, 1996

PMI published the very first *PMBOK® Guide* in 1996. Prior to that, the institute published a white paper called the "Ethics, Standards, and Accreditation Committee Final Report" in the *Project Management Journal®* in 1983 that included baseline standards for the profession. Those standards outlined six major knowledge areas (today there are ten). One of those six was Communications Management.[6]

The very first *PMBOK® Guide* debuted in 1996 with nine knowledge areas, once again including Project Communications Management. The emphasis was on processes that are relatively unilateral—information is disseminated to stakeholders, but there was little acknowledgement of stakeholders having input back into the process. The introduction of the communications section of the guide notably stated, "Everyone involved in the project must be prepared to send and receive communications in the project 'language' and must understand how the communications they are involved in as individuals affect the project as a whole"[7] (as shown in Exhibit 1.1). This put the onus on stakeholders to understand project jargon, which we will discuss more in Chapter 4.

Exhibit 1.1

Quote from the beginning of the Project Communications Management Knowledge Area in the first edition of the PMBOK® Guide

Everyone involved in the project must be prepared to send and receive communications in the project 'language' and must understand how the communications they are involved in as individuals affect the project as a whole.

Additionally, this edition noted, "The general management skill of communicating is related to, but not the same as, project communications management."[8] While some communication concepts were mentioned, such as basic communication models and information delivery techniques, there was no further explanation of the integration of these concepts into the practice of communicating within projects.

The whole of the Project Communications Management Knowledge Area in this first edition comprised just eight pages of the book and was built on four processes, each with inputs, tools and techniques, and outputs:

1. Communications Planning used only one tool: stakeholder analysis. This process included ways to access information in between planned communications, and also acknowledged the need to build in review and revision of the communication plan.
2. Information Distribution was simply what the name of the process implies: the distribution of information about the project to stakeholders.

3. Performance Reporting included status reports (current status), progress reports (what has been done so far), and forecasts (what to expect for the rest of the project).
4. Administrative Closure was the documentation and dissemination of information around the end of each phase of the project and the project as a whole.

Second Edition, 2000

The second edition of the guide expanded the Project Communications Management Knowledge Area by two pages. One interesting change was that the quote noted in Exhibit 1.2 no longer included the phrase "in the project 'language,'" demonstrating that expecting others to understand project jargon was not a viable expectation for the wide range of stakeholders involved in a project.

Exhibit 1.2

Quote from the beginning of the Project Communications Management Knowledge Area in the second edition of the PMBOK® Guide

Everyone involved in the project must be prepared to send and receive communications ~~in the project 'language'~~ and must understand how the communications they are involved in as individuals affect the project as a whole.

The second edition's approach to communications changed relatively little; the most notable changes were some additions within the communications processes. Two outputs were added to the Information Distribution process: project reports and project closures. In the Administrative Closure process, project reports and project presentations were added to tools and techniques, while "formal acceptance" was replaced with "project closure."

Third Edition, 2004

In the third edition, the Project Communications Management Knowledge Area grew to 16 pages, and began to take a more holistic view of communication. While processes were still at the forefront, this version of the guide shifted toward emphasizing the importance of effective communication as a project management skill, rather than implying that stakeholders are responsible for participating in and understanding the importance of project communication. The quote shown in Exhibit 1.3 was modified significantly to, "Everyone involved in the project should understand how communications affect the project as a whole."[9]

Exhibit 1.3

Quote from the beginning of the Project Communications Management Knowledge Area in the third edition of the PMBOK® Guide

~~Everyone involved in the project must be prepared to send and receive communications and must understand how the communications they are involved in as individuals affect the project as a whole.~~

Everyone involved in the project should understand how communications affect the project as a whole.

While the introduction still noted a differentiation between project management communication and general communication skills, it did outline several general communication concepts. Notably, this included an illustration of a basic sender–message–receiver communication model that demonstrated how communication takes place between the party that sends the message and the party that receives it. This model, which has been carried forward through every subsequent revision of the *PMBOK® Guide*, encompassed two important aspects of communication that had not been acknowledged in previous editions: that communication includes some element of feedback to acknowledge that the receiver has received and understood the message, and the concept of "noise" to recognize that many different factors can interfere with transmitting and understanding the message. An understanding of this model is important because, as this edition of the guide now stated, "A breakdown in communications can negatively impact the project."[10]

This emphasis on the importance of communication was carried through in major changes to the processes in the Project Communications Management Knowledge Area in the third edition. The Administrative Closure process was removed and replaced with the Manage Stakeholders process, which focused on communication as a means to "satisfy the requirements of and resolve issues with project stakeholders,"[11] and suggested the connection between good stakeholder management and project success. Changes were also made to the remaining three processes in the knowledge area. These changes broadened the scope of what can affect communication planning, such as enterprise environmental factors (conditions outside the control of the project team, but which can affect the project) and organizational process assets (the knowledge bases and practices of the organization that may be used within the project). The changes also reflected the desired outcome of project communication—to identify and then meet the informational needs of stakeholders, which is an important factor in project success.

Fourth Edition, 2008

The fourth edition of the *PMBOK® Guide* included the single largest increase in the Project Communications Management Knowledge Area across any revision, nearly doubling in size to 29 pages. This edition was the first to directly call out just how significant communication is in a project: "Project managers spend the majority of their time communicating with team members and other project stakeholders, whether they are internal (at all organizational levels) or external to the organization."[12] It also broke down the barrier that previous editions had created between general communication skills and those used in project management: "Most communication skills are common for general management and project management."[13]

Project managers spend the majority of their time communicating.

The four processes from the third edition remained: Plan Communications, Distribute Information, Manage Stakeholder Expectations, and Report Performance. The emphasis on stakeholders increased with the addition of a new process called Identify Stakeholders. It included stakeholder analysis as well as expert judgment and provided examples of tools such as a stakeholder analysis matrix and a power/interest grid. The Manage Stakeholders process was renamed to Manage Stakeholder Expectations, shifting away from the idea of controlling stakeholders and toward the concept of working with them as partners in ensuring project success. Interpersonal and management skills like leadership, influencing, and political/cultural awareness were included as tools for accomplishing this desired outcome.

Fifth Edition, 2013

The fifth edition of the *PMBOK® Guide* brought a major change to the Project Communications Management Knowledge Area. Stakeholder Management was separated out into its own knowledge area, in response to global feedback on the fourth edition regarding the need to expand stakeholder management concepts and recognize communications management and stakeholder management as two distinct areas.[14] As a result, the Identify Stakeholders and Manage Stakeholder Expectations processes were moved to this new knowledge area, reducing the Project Communications Management Knowledge Area to 22 pages.

The three processes that remained in the communications knowledge area were renamed to eliminate confusion and to focus on three key elements:

- Plan Communications Management changed little from the fourth edition.
- Manage Communications (changed from Distribute Information) added an emphasis on the need to ensure that stakeholders understand project communications and have opportunities for further information or clarification.
- Control Communications (changed from Report Performance) emphasized the need for a smooth flow of information among all stakeholders. This process shifted the focus from simply producing reports on how the project is progressing, to ensuring that those reports adequately meet stakeholder needs.

Sixth Edition, 2017

In the most recent edition of the *PMBOK® Guide*, the Project Communications Management Knowledge Area grew substantially, totaling 35 pages. The first sentence of this section shows the shift in the focus from process to purpose, indicating that the processes outlined in this knowledge area are those that are "necessary to ensure that the information needs of the project and its stakeholders are met."[15]

Several key concepts were added to the introduction, including:

- *Key Concepts for Project Communications Management,* which provides definitions, as well as general concepts about how information is exchanged and how miscommunication can be avoided.
- *Trends and Emerging Practices in Project Communications Management,* which looks at recent developments such as the inclusion of stakeholders in project reviews and meetings, and the increasing use of social media and other technology to communicate in projects.
- *Tailoring Considerations,* which includes considerations to apply communication strategies to each unique project.
- *Considerations for Agile/Adaptive Environments,* which for the first time calls out unique considerations for agile projects.

These changes continued the trend toward emphasizing the importance of communication in any project; adapting communication based on the needs of the project, stakeholders, and changing technology/environment; and tying effective project communication to general communication concepts and best practices.

Where We Are Today

Through its iterative revision process, the *PMBOK® Guide* has evolved over time to reflect the developing understanding of the purpose and importance of communication to the practice of project management worldwide. The guide has moved away from being process-oriented and toward acknowledging the important role that communication plays in project success. The guide now offers project managers much more information and knowledge about considerations and proven practices in communication. While this knowledge is not unique to project management, it is crucial in achieving the intent of the Project Communications Management Knowledge Area—to ensure that stakeholders' communication needs are met so that they support the project's deliverables and expected outcomes.

Summary

The goal of this book is to encourage you to think more comprehensively and critically about your project communication, and to view it as much more than a means to provide information to your stakeholders. We hope you will come to see that communication is the most critical factor to project success. In fact, it is *how* the project succeeds by serving as the link between the process (project management) and the people (project stakeholders). By applying the concepts and practices outlined throughout the book, you can plan, manage, and monitor project communications that will not only help your projects succeed, but also help ensure satisfied stakeholders who will contribute toward your positive reputation as an exceptional project participant, regardless of your project role.

As you read this book, consider tailoring the content and concepts to your own project communications practices and approaches. Refer back to the evolution of project communications as you continue to evolve your own project communications. Where we have been will help guide the way to where we are going!

Key Questions

1. What successes and challenges have you experienced when communicating on projects?

2. How would you answer this question: If so much has been written about effective communication in projects, why does ineffective communication continue, risking project success?

3. Now that you have explored the evolution of project communication through the lens of the *PMBOK® Guide*, describe your own journey in communicating on projects. How has your approach to communicating on a project evolved over time?

Notes

1. Kielty (2018).
2. Project Management Institute (2013), *The High Cost of Low Performance*, pp. 1–6.
3. Dominick et al. (2004), p. 5.
4. Carvalho (2013), p. 54.
5. Ziek and Anderson (2015), p. 788.
6. Project Management Institute (1996), *PMBOK® Guide*, 1st ed., p. 139.
7. Project Management Institute (1996), *PMBOK® Guide*, 1st ed., p. 103.
8. Project Management Institute (1996), *PMBOK® Guide*, 1st ed., p. 103.
9. Project Management Institute (2004), *PMBOK® Guide*, 3rd ed., p. 221.
10. Project Management Institute (2004), *PMBOK® Guide*, 3rd ed., p. 224.
11. Project Management Institute (2004), *PMBOK® Guide*, 3rd ed., p. 221.
12. Project Management Institute (2008), *PMBOK® Guide*, 4th ed., p. 243.
13. Project Management Institute (2008), *PMBOK® Guide*, 4th ed., p. 245.
14. Project Management Institute (2013), *PMBOK® Guide*, 5th ed., p. 469.
15. Project Management Institute (2017), *PMBOK® Guide*, 6th ed., p. 359.

References

Carvalho, de M. M. 2013. "An Investigation of the Role of Communication in IT Projects." *International Journal of Operations & Production Management* 34, no. 1, pp. 36–64.

Dominick, P., T. Lechler, and Z. Aronson. 2004. "Project Characteristics and Project Leadership: Understanding Sources of Uncertainty in Project-Based work." *SATM Current Issues in Technology Management* 8, no. 3, pp. 5–7.

Kielty, M. June, 2018. "Robert Trujillo Discusses His Role as Mediator in Metallica." *Ultimate Classic Rock*. https://ultimateclassicrock.com/metallica-mediator-robert-trujillo/

Project Management Institute. 1996. *A Guide to the Project Management Body of Knowledge.* 1st ed. Newtown Square, PA: Project Management Institute.

Project Management Institute. 2000. *A Guide to the Project Management Body of Knowledge.* 2nd ed. Newtown Square, PA: Project Management Institute.

Project Management Institute. 2004. *A Guide to the Project Management Body of Knowledge.* 3rd ed. Newtown Square, PA: Project Management Institute.

Project Management Institute. 2008. *A Guide to the Project Management Body of Knowledge.* 4th ed. Newtown Square, PA: Project Management Institute.

Project Management Institute. 2013. *A Guide to the Project Management Body of Knowledge.* 5th ed. Newtown Square, PA: Project Management Institute.

Project Management Institute. 2017. *A Guide to the Project Management Body of Knowledge.* 6th ed. Newtown Square, PA: Project Management Institute.

Project Management Institute. 2013. *The High Cost of Low Performance: The Essential Role of Communications.* Newtown Square, PA: Project Management Institute.

Rajkumar, S. 2010. "Art of Communication in Project Management." Paper presented at PMI® Research Conference: Defining the Future of Project Management (Washington, DC). Newtown Square, PA: Project Management Institute.

Ziek, P., and J. D. Anderson. 2015. "Communication, Dialogue and Project Management." *International Journal of Managing Projects in Business* 8, no. 4, pp. 788–803.

CHAPTER 2

Exploring Communication Theories

You can't build a great building on a weak foundation. You must have a solid foundation if you're going to have a strong superstructure.[1]
—Gordon B. Hinckley, American religious leader and author

Just like a house needs to be built on a solid foundation, so do project communications. To help establish that foundation, let's take a step back and look at some aspects of communication theory. Why approach project communications from a theoretical standpoint? Understanding *why* people communicate can help demonstrate why communication is so important in projects, and why problems arise when good communication is absent. It can also help you think differently about communication—not just as a process within project management, but as a fundamental driver of collaboration and progress on a project. Looking at project communications through the lens of communication theory can show new ways to improve the effectiveness of your communications, and help you develop new solutions that may prevent or remediate common problems caused by ineffective communication.

For the purpose of this book, we will explore building project communications on the foundation of two communication theories that share some commonality with project environments: uncertainty reduction theory and uncertainty management theory. These theories can help explain *why* the research we reviewed in Chapter 1 says what it does—that effective communication is a critical contributor to project success. With a better understanding of why people communicate, and what happens when they don't, we can see why it is so important to plan, manage, and monitor project communications effectively.

The purpose of this chapter is to help you:

- Understand why people communicate by looking at two different communication theories that focus on communication as a way people handle *uncertainty*
- Evaluate the impact of the quality as well as the quantity of communication in a project
- See the connection between effective communication and stakeholder trust

Communication and Uncertainty

Most project managers and team members will already be familiar with the term uncertainty; typically, however, it is associated with risk management. According to the *PMBOK* Guide, risks are uncertain events or conditions that can affect projects positively or negatively. The process of risk management is oriented toward identifying and managing these uncertainties so that they do not interfere with the accomplishment of project objectives.[2] In the field of communication, however, uncertainty is a cognitive and emotional state that motivates people's actions (or inactions) and behaviors.[3]

In both the communication world and the project world, uncertainty is about not knowing what will happen. In a project, uncertainty affects the project itself—it could positively or negatively impact processes or outcomes of the project. Project uncertainty is evaluated by how far the project could deviate from the plan. It is addressed or managed by considering the likelihood and potential impact of the uncertain condition, and by planning for different strategies and alternatives should the uncertain condition occur. This is addressed in your risk management plan.

When it comes to communication theory, uncertainty affects the *person* rather than the project. An individual evaluates uncertainty based on the *perception* of how it will affect him or her. Perceived consequences can span a wide spectrum. The impact could be concrete, such as, "I made a mistake, and I know that I will be reprimanded by my supervisor." The impact could also be imagined/assumed, such as, "My supervisor does not value my abilities because she did not ask me to participate in this presentation."

Just as project teams use risk management techniques to address the uncertainties in a project, individuals use communication to address the uncertainties in their lives. Think about the initiation of a project. The project team attempts to address many of the uncertainties about the project (for example, estimating cost, schedule, scope, and regulatory or environmental impacts) through project planning and risk identification activities.

> Just as project teams use risk management techniques to address the uncertainties in a project, individuals use communication to address the uncertainties in their lives.

However, the *people* involved in the project harbor uncertainties as well. For example, a member of the project team may be excited about the opportunity to participate, or anxious because this is his first project. He may consider it a chance to show his skills, or he may be frustrated because he already has a lot of work to do and feels he will be overwhelmed by adding the project to his workload. A stakeholder who will be affected by a software implementation may be excited that the new software will make her job easier. Conversely, she may be worried that the software will be difficult to learn and take even more time than the current process.

These uncertainties can motivate actions and behaviors that affect the project. The first-time project team member may jump in enthusiastically and complete his project work early. Or, he may take longer than expected to complete his work because he wants it to be perfect, thereby delaying the project schedule. The stakeholder who will use the new software may serve as an unexpected champion of the project, spreading her positive attitude and getting others excited to use the software. If her reaction is negative, she could spread a resistant attitude toward the software, which could cause problems or delays in adoption when the software rolls out.

So how does a project manager or team member handle these "people-based" uncertainties that can affect the project? This is where an understanding of communication theory can be useful. Let's look at two communication theories that specifically focus on uncertainty, and how people use communication to manage it: uncertainty reduction theory and uncertainty management theory.

Uncertainty Reduction Theory

Uncertainty reduction theory (URT), the older and more well-known of the two theories we will review, defines uncertainty as "having a number of possible alternative predictions or explanations."[4] This theory presumes that people always try to reduce or make sense of uncertainty from a cognitive, information-based perspective. "Making sense of something means increasing your ability to accurately predict or explain it, often by reducing the number of alternative explanations—hopefully to one."[5] Information acquisition, including communication, is the primary means by which people deal with uncertainty.

Two of the main principles of URT can help us understand how uncertainty motivates people to communicate in the context of a project. The first of these principles states that, "Efforts to reduce uncertainty are linked to the likelihood of future interactions and reward potential of the other person."[6] Generally, people are more motivated to reduce uncertainty about another person or situation based on how much influence (both positive and negative) they have over us. A team member who feels that impressing the project manager is beneficial to his status in the organization may ask questions to ensure he is completing his work to expectations. A project manager who does not feel that a particular stakeholder has much influence over the project may put little effort into communicating about the project with that stakeholder.

In your next interaction with a project stakeholder, consider this principle. How does the stakeholder's influence affect the way you communicate with them? We will discuss stakeholder influence more in Chapter 3.

The second principle of URT we will review here explains that people reduce uncertainty through knowledge acquisition. There are three main strategies people use to do this:

1. Passive: Observing other people without actually interacting with them
2. Active: Using indirect methods to collect information about the other person (e.g., conducting an internet search, or asking others about them)
3. Interactive: Seeking information through direct contact with the person (a face-to-face conversation, phone call, e-mail, etc.)[7]

The interactive strategy is the one we most often use day-to-day while doing work on a project. Most planned communication in a project is meant to share information with various stakeholders, thereby increasing their knowledge (and decreasing their uncertainty) about the project. However, planned communications do not always address all stakeholder uncertainties. These unaddressed concerns are often the motivation for stakeholders to reach out to the project team for information (interactive strategy). However, they can also motivate stakeholders to use passive and active strategies to observe or talk to others about the project, potentially making inaccurate assumptions or spreading negative attitudes or misinformation.

Think about this the next time a stakeholder initiates communication with you. What is the purpose of the communication? Is it to acquire knowledge about some aspect of the project? Can you discern any uncertainty the stakeholder has that might have motivated them to reach out to you? Is it information that is needed but was overlooked when planning the project communications?

While this is a brief overview of only two key elements of URT, it sheds some light on what motivates people to communicate within a project. Next, let's look at the second communication theory that focuses on uncertainty.

Uncertainty Management Theory

Uncertainty management theory (UMT) was developed a few decades later. It builds on the work of URT but broadens the impact of uncertainty beyond the cognitive realm to the emotional realm. This addition of the emotional aspect helps explain why, in practice, people do not always attempt to reduce uncertainty.

UMT states that "uncertainty exists when details of situations are ambiguous, complex, unpredictable, or probabilistic; when information is unavailable or inconsistent; and when people feel insecure in their own state of knowledge or the state of knowledge in general."[8] UMT proposes that people react to uncertainty based on how they evaluate the relevance of the uncertainty to their lives, and how they react emotionally to the uncertainty, i.e., do they view it as a threat or as an opportunity?

Under this theory, what determines how people react to, and communicate as a result of, uncertainty? According to Dale Brashers, one of the main developers of the theory, people can respond differently to uncertainty based on both objective evaluation and subjective reaction:

- The person will appraise the likelihood of different outcomes (how likely it is that something will happen or not happen), and how relevant those outcomes will be to them (if this does happen, how will it affect me?). This is similar to the first principle of URT that we shared—motivation to reduce uncertainty is based on the influence and reward potential of the other person. However, UMT broadens this to the relevance of the situation, not just the individual with whom you are communicating. It's also similar in concept to the way that risk analysis is performed, evaluating the significance of the risk by analyzing its probability and impact.

- The person subjectively experiences an *emotional* reaction to the uncertainty that is either positive, negative, or neutral. This is the primary way that UMT differs from URT. A person reacts positively if the uncertainty could be beneficial, or if they tend toward optimism. A person reacts negatively if they perceive danger, and may even panic if the reaction is extreme. Neutral reactions generally occur if the person sees the uncertainty as irrelevant or inconsequential. Finally, it is possible for a person to react both positively and negatively if they perceive both threat and opportunity— think of skydiving or gambling.

In a project, a stakeholder's appraisal of and emotional reaction to uncertainty can help explain the communication actions they take (or do not take):

- Stakeholders may seek information to gain knowledge, or to reinforce or disprove what they already know or believe. They may also seek social support from others as a means to cope with uncertainty. In a project, this can take a positive form when team members share expertise and collaborate to solve a problem or complete a deliverable on time. It could also manifest negatively, as when stakeholders vent frustrations about the project because they are not well-informed of the project status, or because the last project that affected them did not deliver the intended results.

- Team members may also avoid information as a means to shield themselves "from information that is overwhelming and distressing."[9] Avoidance can be conscious or unconscious; mechanisms include direct avoidance, withdrawal, or discounting/discrediting negative information. For example, a team member who is overburdened with project and functional responsibilities may not clarify a task, and instead submit their work with minimal effort. A stakeholder who is distressed about the burdensome impact of a software implementation may avoid reading e-mail communications about the project or not attend a training session.

Table 2.1 shows a high-level comparison of the two theories.

Table 2.1 Comparison of uncertainty reduction and uncertainty management theories

Theory	Uncertainty reduction theory	Uncertainty management theory
Definition of uncertainty	Uncertainty is a cognitive state based on an individual's knowledge, and is separate from emotion.	Uncertainty is both a cognitive (knowledge-based) and emotional state.
Evaluation of uncertainty	Uncertainty is always bad.	Uncertainty could be good or bad.
Behaviors that result from uncertainty	People will communicate in order to reduce uncertainty.	People may or may not communicate to reduce uncertainty based on how they evaluate the probability, impact, and emotional reaction to the uncertainty.

Uncertainty and Effective Communication

As a project manager, how do you tackle these stakeholder uncertainties that can impact your project? Through communication! Specifically, by communicating enough (quantity) and by communicating well (quality). Let's look at both of these aspects.

Quantity of Communication

People can't act on, or react to, information they do not have. If information is a primary way to reduce or manage uncertainty, lack of communication limits stakeholders' ability to make sense of the situation and make decisions about how to think, feel, and act. Often they fill in the gaps with assumptions, or they may speak negatively about the project out of frustration. The more they are invested in or affected by the project, the more they are likely to make assumptions and share those assumptions with peers, such as spreading gossip or rumors.

Quantity of information doesn't necessarily mean sending more e-mails—most workers already feel like their inboxes are flooded. But you do need to ensure information is available to people when and how they need it. We will address ways to do this in the next two chapters, where we discuss audience communication preferences (see Chapter 3), and basic guidelines and considerations for project communications (see Chapter 4).

Another aspect to consider is that communication is not all verbal; in fact, much of it is not. A significant amount of meaning is communicated through physical cues (facial expressions and body language) and voice (tone, inflection, and other vocal cues outside of the words themselves). This means that communications you are delivering through methods that use only text or voice will have reduced effectiveness. We'll look at this further in Chapter 4.

Virtual teams especially can be impacted by this. When there is limited face-to-face interaction, even via methods such as video calls, teams can struggle to develop an effective approach to working together because the opportunities to reduce uncertainty are decreased. If the vast majority of the team's interactions are, in fact, virtual, the team will need to work harder to compensate for the lack of nonverbal communication.

Quality of Communication

High-quality communication gets your message across clearly and effectively. For example, consider the word "dog." What image comes to mind? One person might envision a golden retriever, while another person pictures a chihuahua. A third might picture the mutt that was a beloved family pet from childhood. They're all thinking of a dog, but the dogs they are picturing are very different. Ferdinand de Saussure, a linguist who was one of the founders of the field of semiotics, called these distinctions the *signifier* (the word itself—in this example, "dog") and the *signified* (the mental concept—in this example, the image your mind conjures of a dog).

How does this apply to project communications? Suppose an assignment within the project is to research similar projects to learn what technologies might be useful. The project manager giving the assignment might mean "research" as a very thorough and exhaustive process of seeking out all available options and carefully weighing the pros and cons of each. For the team member assigned this task, however, it might mean a cursory search to find evidence that supports what he already thinks or wants to do.[10] To a stakeholder, "soon" could mean 2 hours, but to you it could mean tomorrow.

Quality communication requires that the person sending the message must make sure that the message he or she wants to send is accurately received. One way to do this is to be clear and specific about what you are communicating. If you need a task completed by 3 p.m. tomorrow, don't just say "tomorrow afternoon." When communicating an assignment or request, provide as much SMART[11] information as you can:

- **S**pecific: What is the scope of what needs to be done? Make sure the assignment is clearly defined.
- **M**easurable: How will you determine completion/success? State any metrics or parameters for measuring and tracking progress.
- **A**ttainable: Is what you are asking attainable in the parameters given? Ask for feedback on this from the team member(s) involved.
- **R**elevant: Have you tied the task to the overall project goals? Ensure team members involved understand why this task is important.
- **T**ime-bound: What is the deadline for this task? Be as precise as you can.

Another way to communicate clearly is to limit your use of vocabulary that is not universally understood, a.k.a. jargon. Project management uses a lot of technical terminology; just a few examples are "critical path," "free float," and "lag," not to mention acronyms like EVM, LOE, and RACI. Be conscious that many stakeholders and even team members who are new to project management may not understand these terms. We'll talk more about the issues that can arise from using jargon in Chapter 4.

A third way to ensure quality of communication is to seek feedback from the receiver to verify that they understood what you intended to communicate. You can consider feedback a means of quality assurance in your communications. We'll look more at this concept in Chapter 6.

Reducing Uncertainty Builds Trust

Why use communication to help eliminate uncertainty with project stakeholders? Uncertainty is closely tied to trust. When you think about whether you trust someone, what factors do you consider? Most people count honesty (presenting information accurately and truthfully) and reliability (doing what you say you will do) as major factors in trusting others. Both factors speak to the level of uncertainty you have about the other person's words and resultant behaviors.

In a team environment like a project, trust is critical to success. Trust results in high-functioning teams that exhibit dedication to successful project outcomes and are often willing to take personal risks to advance common goals.[12] It also results in stakeholders that develop and maintain support for the project and the project team. We'll talk more about stakeholder support in Chapter 3.

On the other hand, there are consequences when a team lacks trust. It's not just about reduced performance; it is a cycle that feeds itself. Just as good communication cultivates trust, lack of trust can lead to poor communication. "In lack of trust, members may delay communication, or reduce quality of communication by giving insufficient knowledge and misinforming. So team trust supports to healthier and more reliable formal communication in teams."[13] Similarly, stakeholders who do not trust the project team can withhold support and even delay or derail the project entirely.

As business leader and author Stephen R. Covey has stated, trust is "the most essential ingredient in effective communication. It's the foundational principle that holds all relationships."[14] Build a solid foundation for your project by establishing trust with your stakeholders through effective communication.

Summary

Project communication starts by building on a solid foundation—an understanding through communication theory of why people communicate, and what happens when they communicate ineffectively. Two communication theories that apply well to project communications are URT and UMT. These theories view uncertainty as a primary motivation to communicate (or not to communicate). People use communication as a tool to gain information that will reduce their uncertainty.

Understanding uncertainty as a motivator can help project managers and stakeholders appreciate the value of communication as a means to manage uncertainty, and therefore manage the project. Two ways to manage uncertainty are to ensure sufficient quantity and high quality of communications. These strategies for good communication can help build trust among project team members and outside stakeholders, which is a key factor in project success.

Key Questions

1. In your opinion, what are the similarities and differences between the way uncertainty is defined in communication theory and in project management? Discuss your findings with other stakeholders, colleagues, or classmates.

2. How does a stakeholder's influence affect the way you communicate with them? In your next stakeholder interaction, document your experience.

3. Select an opportunity where a stakeholder initiates communication with you. Can you discern any uncertainty that might have motivated the stakeholder to reach out to you? Is it an uncertainty you could have addressed in your project communications management plan?

Notes

1. Gordon Hinckley.com, https://gordonhinckley.com/about.
2. Project Management Institute (2017), *PMBOK® Guide* 6th ed., p. 397.
3. Greene and Burleson (2003), p. 942.
4. Redmond (2015), p. 4.
5. Redmond (2015), p. 7.
6. Redmond (2015), p. 11.
7. Redmond (2015), pp. 16–18.
8. Brashers (2001), p. 478.
9. Brashers (2001), p. 484.
10. Hiyashi (2011), p. 35.
11. Doran (1981), p. 35-36.
12. Sinek (2009), p. 118.
13. Polat et al. (2018), p. 101.
14. Kruse (2012).

References

Bradac, J. 2001. "Theory Comparison: Uncertainty Reduction, Problematic Integration, Uncertainty Management, and Other Curious Constructs." *Journal of Communication*, 51, no. 3, pp. 456–475.

Brashers, D. E. 2001. "Communication and Uncertainty Management." *Journal of Communication*, 51, no. 3, 477–497. doi:10.1111/j.1460-2466 .2001.tb02892.x

Covey, S. M. R., and R. R. Merrill. 2006. *The Speed of Trust: The One Thing That Changes Everything*. New York: Free Press.

Doran, G. T. 1981. "There's a S.M.A.R.T. way to write management's goals and objectives" *Management Review*, 70, no. 11, 35–36.

DuFrene, D. D., and C. M. Lehman. 2016. *Managing Virtual Teams*, 2nd ed. New York: Business Expert Press.

GordonHinckley.com. "About." https://gordonhinckley.com/about, (accessed September 23, 2019).

Greene, J. O. and B. R. Burleson, eds. 2003. *Handbook of Communication and Social Interaction Skills*. Mahwah, NJ: Lawrence Erlbaum Associates.

Hayashi, S. K. 2011. *Conversations for Change.* New York: McGraw Hill.

Kruse, K. July, 2012. "Stephen Covey: 10 Quotes That Can Change Your Life." *Forbes,* https://www.forbes.com/sites/kevinkruse/2012/07/16/the-7-habits/#2712a1b839c6

Polat, V., Gary L., Ali E. A., and O. E. Onat. 2018. "Formal and Informal Communication in New Product Development Teams: The Mediation Effect of Team Trust." *International Journal of Innovation* 6, no. 2, pp. 97–111.

Project Management Institute. 2017. *A Guide to the Project Management Body of Knowledge.* 6th ed. Newtown Square, PA: Project Management Institute.

Redmond, M. V. 2015. "Uncertainty Reduction Theory." Iowa State University Digital Repository. English Technical Reports and White Papers, 3, http://lib.dr.iastate.edu/engl_reports/3

Sinek, S. 2009. *Start with Why: How Great Leaders Inspire Everyone to Take Action.* London: Portfolio.

CHAPTER 3

Knowing Your Audience

Seek first to understand, then to be understood.[1]
—Steven R. Covey, American educator, author, and
business leader

Say you have been asked to make a presentation to a group about project management (or any topic on which you have some level of expertise). One of the most critical pieces of information you need in order to prepare your speech is to know your audience—who you are delivering it to. Consider how differently you would deliver your message to a group of 10-year-olds at a school career day; students in a college graduate program; the executive leadership team of your project; or a neighborhood group looking to build a new community center.

No matter what the method of communication—presentation, e-mail, phone call, status report—it's important to know who will be receiving your message. When you tailor your communication to your audience, they are more likely to understand and respond appropriately. This concept is called *audience design*—altering the way you are delivering your message to suit the communication needs and expectations of those to whom you are communicating. A clear understanding of the audience and what matters to them will result in more effective communication, more active stakeholder engagement, and, ultimately, a more successful project.

The purpose of this chapter is to help you:

- Explore various recommendations for identifying the audience in your project, including their role, their level of power and influence over the project, and their level of support for the project
- See the value of understanding what is important to the members of your audience—the WIIFM (what's in it for me)

- Become familiar with stakeholder personas as a communication approach
- Put it into practice: Know your audience in traditional, agile, and virtual project teams

Audience = Stakeholders

In a project, the audience is the stakeholders, defined by the *PMBOK®* *Guide* as "an individual, group, or organization that may affect, be affected by, or perceive itself to be affected by a decision, activity, or outcome of a project, program, or portfolio."[2]

Stakeholders have become an increasingly important concept in project management, so much so that Stakeholder Management was separated out into its own knowledge area in the fifth edition of the *PMBOK®* *Guide* released in 2013. This change was in response to feedback around the need to expand stakeholder management concepts and recognize communications management and stakeholder management as two distinct areas.[3] Prior to the fifth edition, concepts around stakeholder management were mainly covered in the Project Communications Management Knowledge Area.

Why is it important to take a thorough look at your project's stakeholders? Because in many ways, stakeholders *are* the project. The project cannot be completed without those who initiate it, execute it, and live with the results once the project is complete. You can have a project without a charter, or a risk management plan, or a work breakdown structure. But you cannot have a project without stakeholders. Stakeholders can also be the barometer by which project success is measured—stakeholder satisfaction is one of the criteria outlined in the *PMBOK®* *Guide* for assessing project success. If stakeholders are not satisfied with the project outcomes, it may not matter whether you have fully achieved the project's objectives. And research shows that consideration for stakeholders only continues to grow within the field of project management.[4]

It's clear that stakeholders are important. Now, let's look at how to figure out who they are in your project, and what you need to know about them in order to effectively communicate with them.

Identifying Stakeholders

The Project Stakeholder Management Knowledge Area of the *PMBOK®
Guide* outlines a process for determining who is a stakeholder in your
project. Many of a project's stakeholders can be discerned by reviewing
project documents, including the charter, business case, and agreements.
Another tool for identifying stakeholders in a project is expert judgment,
which includes seeking input from:

- Those who have a thorough understanding of the organization's
  functions, culture, and power structures. These people can help
  identify stakeholders who may have interest in or influence over
  the project.
- Those with thorough knowledge of the industry, customers, or
  wider environment. They can help identify stakeholders and stakeholder concerns that derive from the external environment in
  which the project will exist.

Remember that some stakeholders will be easy to identify, such as the
sponsor and the team. It may be more difficult, however, to identify *everyone* who will be impacted by the project. The information presented here is
intended to give you a starting point for identifying stakeholders and their
characteristics to help you communicate with them more effectively; however, it is not intended to be an exhaustive guide to identifying project stakeholders. Further, your list of stakeholders may change over the course of the
project as new stakeholders come to light, or as changes to the project bring
changes to your list of stakeholders. The *PMBOK® Guide* recommends reviewing and updating your stakeholder engagement plan routinely, especially as the project moves from one phase to another, and when there are
changes in the project's stakeholder community or within the organization.[5]

As you identify your project stakeholders, keep track of them using
a tool such as a stakeholder register. You can find a template for a stakeholder register in Table 3.2 later in this chapter. Some of the information
you will want to track includes the role(s) the stakeholder plays in the
project and the organization; the stakeholder's power and influence; and
the stakeholder's level of support for the project.

Roles

Roles include the person or group's position within the organization as well as their relationship to the project. Roles include titles or descriptors like project manager, business partner, sponsor, subject matter expert, business analyst, etc. For example, in a software implementation project, the head of IT in the organization will certainly be a stakeholder, as will any employees expected to use the new software. Roles are an excellent starting point for building your stakeholder register, and for understanding how you can best communicate with each individual or group.

Power and Influence

Two key factors to understand about each of your stakeholder groups are their level of power and their influence. Power is a representation of the stakeholder's level of authority as it relates to the project. For example, a project sponsor has the ability to stop or completely shut down the project, so they have a very high level of power with regard to the project. An end user who will be using the new product or software generated by the project, for example, may have a relatively low level of power.

Influence, which is often related to power, is an indicator of how much the stakeholder can affect others involved with the project. Who can they influence, and how strongly? The software's end users may not have a high level of power, but they still have the ability to spread negative views about the project, which can influence others' support for the project, as well as the long-term adoption and integration of the project outcomes into the organization.

One way to categorize stakeholder influence is by defining their "direction" of influence, as shown in Table 3.1.

Table 3.1 Stakeholder direction of influence[6]

Direction of influence	Those influenced (other stakeholder groups)
Upward	Senior management, sponsor, steering committee
Downward	Those working on the project
Outward	Stakeholders outside the project, including vendors, customers, or end users
Sideward	Peers, including other project managers and colleagues who have a similar level of power/influence

Support

Stakeholder support can make or break a project. In the section on planning stakeholder engagement, the *PMBOK® Guide* offers five classifications of stakeholder engagement:

- **Unaware**: Stakeholders who are unaware do not know of the project's existence. They do not have the basic knowledge required to move to a different classification of engagement.
- **Resistant**: Resistant stakeholders know about the project but do not support it. They may actively work to stop the project in whole or in part.
- **Neutral**: Stakeholders who are neutral do not act in ways that either promote or detract from the project. Often these stakeholders are not highly impacted by the project.
- **Supportive**: Supportive stakeholders take steps to support the project in words and/or actions.
- **Leading**: These stakeholders take a leadership role in ensuring the project succeeds.[7]

One way to look at these classifications is on a spectrum, as shown in Figure 3.1. Keep in mind that stakeholders can move in either direction on this spectrum. A resistant stakeholder can move toward being more supportive; likewise a supportive stakeholder can move toward being resistant. Communication (or lack thereof) is a powerful tool in moving stakeholders along the spectrum.

Figure 3.1 The spectrum of stakeholder engagement

In your stakeholder engagement planning, you should attempt to identify where each of your stakeholders are on this spectrum, and where they need to be in order for the project to progress smoothly and achieve its goals. Why is this important? Because knowing where your stakeholders sit on this spectrum can help you and the project team develop and implement communication strategies that align with stakeholders' expectations and interests.

A good stakeholder engagement plan starts with identifying who your stakeholders are, their role, power and influence in the project, and their current and desired levels of support for the project. The next step is understanding how to engage your stakeholders in order to keep them informed and move them toward the level of support needed for the project to succeed.

What's in It for Me?

Identifying the project stakeholders and their relationship to the project is the first step. To be able to communicate with them most effectively, you must understand what these stakeholders care about. In other words, what are their *stakes* in your project?

Frequently referred to as "what's in it for me" or WIIFM, this concept is basic but powerful. Simply put, people respond better and engage more when you talk about what matters to them. This is especially true when you want them to take action, or when you're asking them to support changes that disrupt their "business as usual." The WIIFM is the value proposition of the project for each stakeholder or group.

> The WIIFM is the value proposition of the project for each stakeholder or group.

After all, "just as the stakeholders may affect the project, the project affects stakeholders."[8] Stakeholders want to know how the project will impact them, when it will happen, and what kind of support they will receive in adjusting to the changes the project brings. A project team member might care most about what will be expected of them and who they will be working with. The project sponsor might want to know about factors that impact whether the project will deliver its intended results, and the project's priority within the organization.

All of these elements are—you guessed it!—uncertainties. How will the project affect them? What are the expectations for them, both during the project and once it has been completed? Is there anything about the project that might negatively impact them? The more you can learn about what kind of impact the project will or could have on your different stakeholder groups, the better you can communicate to reduce their uncertainty about it, and increase their support for it.

Finding the WIIFM

When it comes to project stakeholders, how do you know what matters to them? What are they uncertain about? A good place to start is to simply put yourself in their shoes. Take your list of stakeholders and imagine how you would feel as a team member, a sponsor, a subject matter expert, a functional manager, end user, etc. What would be most important to you? Would you be concerned that the project could affect your status in the organization, either positively or negatively, or the way you do your work? If you are a functional manager, you might be concerned with whether your employee's time on the project will impact his or her regular duties. If you are the IT department head during a software implementation, you may have a number of concerns, ranging from compatibility with other company software, to resource allocation, to responsibility for training and supporting the new software once the implementation is complete.

Some of these considerations will be easy to discern on your own. But others may be less obvious. An executive sponsor may have recently had a bad experience with another project exceeding its deadline, so he is skeptical of whether this project will be delivered on time. A functional manager may have staff working on several other projects in addition to this one, so she may be resistant to the idea of one more project taking up her staff's time.

The *PMBOK® Guide's* process of identifying stakeholders includes methods to collect additional data about stakeholders and their interests, such as surveys and brainstorming meetings with the project team. If you're using expert judgment, as previously noted, this can also be a valuable tool for identifying not only who your stakeholders are, but what their concerns are about the project.

Meetings are another technique that can be useful with a wide range of stakeholder types and groups, especially when done early on in the project. In fact, face-to-face or virtual meetings can be invaluable in understanding stakeholder concerns because you will be able to learn from nonverbal communication as well (see Chapter 4). These meetings can also bring to the surface concerns or even identify new stakeholder groups that the project team may have missed.

When talking with stakeholders to understand their interests in the project, ask basic questions like:

- On a scale of 1 to 10 (where 1 is extremely low and 10 is extremely high), how impactful is this project on your day-to-day work?
- What do you see as the biggest benefit of this project?
- Is there anything about this project that worries you?
- Are there aspects of this project that conflict with your other priorities?

Don't debate the feedback you receive. The goal of these conversations isn't to win anyone over; it is simply to develop a fuller understanding of their concerns about the project, and to show stakeholders that you are motivated to understand and address these concerns. Keep in mind, however, that if you take the time—both yours and the stakeholders'—to learn about their concerns, you will need to ensure that what you learn is somehow addressed within your project plan and project communications. Learning their concerns is a great way to build trust, but doing nothing with that information is a sure way to lose it.

Add all of the data you collect to your stakeholder register. It should have a robust and nuanced "WIIFM" field for every stakeholder group that covers everything you have learned in your identification of stakeholders. Table 3.2 shows a stakeholder register template that includes the stakeholders you have identified, their role, power, influence, level of support, and their WIIFM. You can modify this template to add other factors that can help characterize and understand your stakeholders based on the unique elements of each particular project. When crafting your messaging

Table 3.2 Stakeholder register template

Stakeholder	Role	Power	Influence	Support	WIIFM
Stakeholder 1					
Stakeholder 2					
Stakeholder 3					

to stakeholders, incorporate these considerations into *what* you say and *how* you say it. Your communications will be more effective when your stakeholders see that you know, understand, and address their concerns.

Segmentation and Personas

Audience segmentation is a marketing concept where customers are divided into groups based on similar demographics, needs, preferences, and buying potential, similar to the process of analyzing stakeholders and grouping them based on similar characteristics. In marketing, this plays out in how and where products are advertised to maximize resources. For example:

- A technology company releasing a new, cutting-edge gadget might advertise through websites or magazines that specifically target early technology adopters.
- A company that sells soft drinks might want to target many different markets, but they customize their messaging to different groups and deliver that messaging through channels targeting those groups.
  - One advertisement showing younger people drinking the product while having fun by a swimming pool might be advertised during television shows favored by this group.
  - Meanwhile, a separate advertisement depicting multiple generations of a family drinking the beverage around the dinner table might be shown during family-oriented television programming.

It's a way of meeting the customer where they are and showing them what's in it for them.

While the concept of segmentation has been around for quite some time, a more recent development is the use of customer personas when targeting audience segments. This idea first originated within software design to represent archetypal users of the software or system, and was quickly adopted by the marketing field to inform how messages should be tailored to customer segments. A persona is a single fictional character that represents the synthesis of all of the relevant characteristics of those who make up a customer (or stakeholder) segment.

Personas may be a useful approach to help you craft your messaging for some of your stakeholder groups, especially in larger projects where stakeholder segments might include a large number of people. With large stakeholder groups it may be difficult to keep all of their concerns organized. A persona allows you to capture all of the characteristics of each group so that you can craft and deliver your messages most effectively.

Personas are usually drafted as a character sketch of one to two pages. Table 3.3 contains a template for helping you create stakeholder personas, along with questions to consider.

Table 3.3 Stakeholder persona template

Stakeholder name:		
Characteristics	Organizational role Role within the project Reporting structure	• What are the organizational characteristics of the group, which may include their role/position, their relationship to the project in terms of power and influence, reporting structures, etc.? • What characteristics have already been identified in the stakeholder analysis?
Support	Current level of support Desired level of support	• What is their current level of support for the project—unaware, resistant, neutral, supportive, or leading? • What is their desired level of support for project success?
Motivations	Top organizational priorities WIIFM Positive impacts of the project	• What is this group's top priorities, interests, and goals? How does the project fit into that? • What is their "WIIFM" in relation to this project? • In what ways might the project positively affect them?

Barriers	Uncertainties Negative impacts of the project	• What are their uncertainties about the project? • Are there ways in which the project might negatively impact them (whether real or perceived)? • What other factors might negatively affect their support for the project?
Communication Preferences	Project communication needs Current communication methods	• What are the most important factors about the project that this group needs to be informed of, and when? • What current communication methods does this group already use, that can be employed to deliver communications about the project?

Give the persona a name. This can be an actual person's name, such as John Brown, or a categorical name, such as end users. Personal names may help keep a more "human" perspective of the stakeholder group by reminding the project team that the persona represents real people who are affected by the project and need to be communicated with.

Incorporate your personas into your project communications management plan (see Chapter 5). When crafting and delivering your messages, these personas can help ensure that you are telling the right stakeholders the right information, the right way, at the right time.

Putting It into Practice

Here are a few practical tips, fun activities, and useful ideas for how you can implement the concepts in this chapter into your project environment. Note that ideas listed in one type of team may be adapted to other teams. Be creative. Use these as a starting point. Add your own ideas to build your communications toolkit.

Knowing your audience	
Traditional project teams	• Encourage team members to meet in a less formal setting (e.g., coffee, tea, or lunch) to get to know one another and to learn from each other. • As the project manager, interview each team member prior to the start of the project to get to know them. • For each key stakeholder group, assign specific team members to research their background (company annual report, website, executive team, what they do, business core values, etc.) and give a presentation to the rest of the team. Post the presentation on the project website for ease of reference.
Agile project teams	• Invite stakeholders to a stand-up meeting to demonstrate how the team operates. • Revisit your stakeholder analysis at the beginning of each sprint. As the project iterates and evolves, additional stakeholder groups may need to be incorporated into your project and project communications management plans. • Try creating personas for a few of your large stakeholder groups using the template in Table 3.3. Ask the entire team to contribute to this exercise, so that they are engaged in the process and more likely to consider how these personas are affected by the project and what their communication needs will be.
Virtual project teams	• Post a map on a "virtual wall" and have each team member pinpoint their location and share a photo of their home or work environment. • Consider using an icebreaker (e.g., What is your favorite television show, or What is your hobby?) at the start of virtual team meetings to encourage team members to get to know one another. • As a team, discuss where each of your stakeholders fall on the engagement spectrum: unaware, resistant, neutral, supportive, or leading. Create a visual representation of your findings and post it on your virtual team wall for easy reference.

Summary

Every stakeholder is a member of your audience. When communicating, it is critical to know your audience. It is also important to know how several factors about your audience can impact their engagement with your communications—and your project!

Communication strategies may need to be adjusted based on stakeholders' roles (their position in the organization and functional relationship to the project), power (their level of authority as it relates to the project), and influence (how much the stakeholder can affect others involved in the project or the organization). There are five categories of stakeholder engagement: unaware, resistant, neutral, supportive, and leading. Knowing where your stakeholders are on this spectrum can help you and the project team develop and implement communication strategies that align with stakeholder expectations and interests.

Understanding what stakeholders care about starts with WIIFM, or "what's in it for me." The WIIFM is the value proposition of the project for each stakeholder or group. When working with a large group of stakeholders, consider developing stakeholder personas to capture all of a stakeholder group's characteristics and concerns. This can help you craft and deliver your message most effectively to stakeholder groups that contain a large number of people.

Identifying your audience, understanding what their stakes are in the project, and considering the factors that can influence how they receive and perceive communication can help make your project communications much more effective. The end result: decreased uncertainty, increased trust, and improved chances for project success!

Key Questions

1. Describe your experience in communicating with stakeholders. What situations have been the most successful and/or the most challenging? What advice would you give to new project managers in communicating with stakeholders?

2. Using the five classifications of stakeholder engagement, what communication strategies would you use to move a stakeholder from a position of resisting your project to a more supportive role?

3. Working with your project team, develop stakeholder personas using the template provided. What categories or questions would you add? What value do you see in using stakeholder personas?

Notes

1. Covey, accessed September 23, 2019, https://www.franklincovey
   .com/the-7-habits/habit-5.html.
2. Project Management Institute (2017), *PMBOK® Guide* 6th ed., p. 723.
3. Project Management Institute (2013), *PMBOK® Guide* 5th ed., p. 469.
4. Littau et al. (2010), p. 17.
5. Project Management Institute (2017), *PMBOK® Guide* 6th ed., p. 505.
6. Project Management Institute (2017), *PMBOK® Guide* 6th ed., p. 513.
7. Project Management Institute (2017), *PMBOK® Guide* 6th ed., p. 521.
8. Huemann et al. (2016), p. 43.

References

Bourne, L. and S. Kasperczyk. 2009. "Introducing a Stakeholder Management Methodology into the EU." Paper presented at PMI® Global Congress 2009—EMEA (Amsterdam, The Netherlands), Newtown Square, PA: Project Management Institute. https://www.pmi.org/learning/library/introducing-stakeholder-circle-methodology-6844

Cooper, A. 2019. "The Origin of Personas." *Cooper Professional Education.* https://www.cooper.com/journal/2008/05/the_origin_of_personas/, (accessed September 11, 2019).

Covey, S. R. 2019. "Habit 5: Seek First to Understand, Then to Be Understood." FranklinCovey.com. https://www.franklincovey.com/the-7-habits/habit-5.html, (accessed September 23, 2019).

DuFrene, D. D., and C. M. Lehman. 2016. *Managing Virtual Teams.* 2nd ed. New York: Business Expert Press.

Hall, E. T. 1976. *Beyond Culture.* New York, NY: Doubleday.

Horton, W. S., and Spieler, D. H. 2007. "Age-Related Differences in Communication and Audience Design." *Psychology and Aging* 22, no. 2, pp. 281–290. doi:10.1037/0882-7974.22.2.281.

Huemann, M., P. Eskerod, and C. Ringhofer. 2016. *Rethink! Project Stakeholder Management.* Newtown Square, PA: Project Management Institute.

Littau, P., N. J. Jujagiri, and G. Adlbrecht. 2010. "25 Years of Stakeholder Theory in Project Management Literature (1984–2009)." *Project Management Journal*, 41, no. 4, pp. 17–29.

Paulston, C. B., S. F. Kiesling, and E. S. Rangel, eds. 2012. *The Handbook of Intercultural Discourse and Communication*. West Sussex, UK: Wiley-Blackwell.

Phillips, M. 2014. *Reinventing Communication: How to Design, Lead and Manage High Performing Projects*. Surrey, UK: Gower Publishing.

Project Management Institute. 2013. *A Guide to the Project Management Body of Knowledge*. 5th ed. Newtown Square, PA: Project Management Institute.

Project Management Institute. 2017. *A Guide to the Project Management Body of Knowledge*. 6th ed. Newtown Square, PA: Project Management Institute.

St. Louis, M. September 21, 2017. "How to Create Customer Personas that Breathe Life into Your Marketing." *Inc.com*, https://www.inc.com/molly-reynolds/how-to-create-customer-personas-that-brealife-into-your-marketing.html.

Wowk, R. May 11, 2018. "Using Stakeholder Personas to Understand Internal Stakeholders." *Picklejar Communications*, http://www.picklejarcommunications.com/2018/05/11/using-personas-to-understand-internal-stakeholders/.

CHAPTER 4

Starting with the Basics

We have two ears and one mouth so that we can listen twice as much as we speak.[1]

—Epictetus, Greek philosopher

So far we have learned about uncertainty and getting to know your audience. Now we're ready to start with the basics—the foundation for project communications.

There are many books and resources available on the basics of communication. Many of these same basic principles apply to communicating on projects. Some fundamental techniques will be outlined in this chapter, while some are explored further in other chapters. This chapter will focus on the basic tenets of good communication that will help project managers, team members, and project sponsors be effective communicators.

The purpose of this chapter is to help you:

- Look at how high-performing organizations and project teams communicate
- Identify things to consider when communicating on projects, including the need for inclusive language
- Distinguish between formal and informal communications
- Examine the scalability of project communications
- Put it into practice: Project communication basics in traditional, agile, and virtual project teams

Other chapters have additional insights on this topic as well, and Appendix B has more resources and communication books for your reference. We encourage you to also refer to other resources for "general" or "business" communication principles and practices. Our focus here is on *project* communications.

When it comes to communications, what do high-performing organizations do differently than other organizations? In PMI's "The High Cost of Low Performance: The Essential Role of Communications" report, their findings show that high-performing organizations:

- communicate key project topic areas better, including the objective of the project, its value for the business, and its outcomes, along with budget, scope, and schedule;
- are better at delivering clear, detailed communications about the project on time, through appropriate channels, with nontechnical language;
- use formal communications plans for nearly twice as many projects as low-performing organizations;
- create project communications management plans that are more than three times as effective as the plans of low-performing organizations.[2]

As you can see, high-performing organizations communicate effectively and use formal communications plans in their projects. In Chapter 5, we will discuss more about project communications management plans. In this chapter, we will look at some of the basic elements of effective communications in projects.

To get started on thinking about how you can establish a solid foundation for your project communications, let's begin with a few questions. (By the way, asking questions is an excellent project communications technique to use!)

- As communicators, how can we become more like these high-performing organizations, and become a high-performing project team?
- What does effective communication look like? Does it vary by situations, cultures, experiences, or different types of project teams?
- What elements of project communications are the most challenging?

- How does communicating with individuals within the project team differ from communicating with stakeholders outside the team?
- What do we need to consider when communicating at different levels in the organization?

Keep these questions, and your answers, in mind as you read on. You may have other questions to add as we begin to explore the basics in project communications.

Project Communications Basics: Things to Consider

Things certainly have changed in the way we communicate. Rarely do we use conventional methods of communicating like postal mail, interoffice memo, landline telephone, and facsimile. With project team members located around the world and the desire for instant information, there is a dramatic increase in the use of electronic devices, social media, cloud communication, and technology. Regardless of how you communicate on projects, there is one thing that hasn't changed—the basics. Let's begin with a brief overview of some basic principles as well as actions to consider when communicating on projects. Add items from your own experiences as well. Plus, you can refer to Chapter 7 for more on communication tools and to Appendix B for additional resources.

Words Matter

In a leadership role—in projects, business, or other environments—people may hang on to every word you say. Words have an impact. Your words may have a positive impact that encourages and inspires the project team, or your words may have a negative impact where team members "shut down" and resist getting tasks done.

Choose your words carefully, both in writing and orally. You never know what lasting impact, good or bad, your words may have.

> Choose your words carefully. You never know what lasting impact your words may have.

Verbal and Nonverbal Communication

As mentioned in Chapter 2, not all communication is verbal or written. There is also tone—the volume or inflection of the words being said. Most important, however, is what is *not* being said—the body language. This includes facial expressions, eye contact, movement of hands, position of arms and legs, and other factors. Much research has been done (with varying results) on how much of our communication is done through body language. Many scholars conclude that body language makes up a significant percentage of our communication. This makes it especially challenging in working with virtual teams because you are not able to *see* team members' body language when you are having a conversation (without using video or a camera device). You must rely mostly on the *words* being said. Understanding body language and the ability to "read" the nonverbal signals or movements are key skills for communicating on projects.

Listen

Do you listen differently when you are communicating with external stakeholders versus internal project team members? Do you listen more intently when a customer is talking rather than when a colleague is speaking? Listening differently often happens on project teams. Internally, most often the team member does not report to the project manager. Usually, the team member reports directly to a supervisor or functional manager. So why should the team member listen to the project manager, if they don't report to them? How do you get an executive stakeholder to listen to you when you have little or no authority?

Active listening is an important skill for everyone on the project. The Center for Creative Leadership (CCL), a nonprofit educational institution which focuses on leadership development, has identified six key active listening skills:

1. Be attentive.
2. Keep an open mind.
3. Be attuned to and reflect feelings.

4. Ask open-ended and probing questions.
5. Paraphrase.
6. Share your own thoughts and feelings.[3]

In your next communication interaction or project team meeting, intentionally put these six active listening skills to use.

Give and Seek Feedback

While listening is important, receiving feedback is equally important. Bill Gates once said, "We all need people who will give us feedback. That's how we improve."[4] Feedback allows you to make necessary adjustments. For example, you distribute a weekly status report via e-mail on Monday afternoon. Team members are then expected to provide their comments on the status report at the weekly team meeting on Tuesday morning. However, a few members of the project team often do not get a chance to read the report and prepare their comments in that short turnaround time, and as a result the team meetings are not as effective as they could be. By asking for feedback on communication methods, the team members can bring this issue to the attention of the project manager. The project manager can then take action—possibly choosing to adjust the timing of the status report distribution or the team meeting—to allow all team members to contribute more effectively.

Feedback allows you to confirm that the communication methods you are using are working and adjust those methods that are not working. Or, if a method is working for some but not others, remember that you don't have to get rid of what you have. Rather, you can add a communication method that can support all stakeholders. Feedback on communication processes helps identify potential communication breakdowns before or as soon as they occur. Look for opportunities where you can provide feedback—both as a way to recognize a job well done, and areas where improvement is needed. We will discuss feedback more in Chapter 6.

Deal with "Talkers"

Do you have people on your project team who love to hear themselves talk? These individuals are usually creating *and* sharing their thoughts at the same time, rather than formulating their thoughts first before speaking. They use "airtime" and seem to never get to the point. One technique to try is the talking spoon; or use any object that you can hold in your hand. A pencil, pen, or marker will also work. The object gives you permission to talk. As long as you are holding the object, it is your turn to speak. When you are done talking, you put the object down on the table, and another person picks up the object. It is now their turn to speak, and it is your turn to listen. This exercise can be done informally without others even knowing it. Or it can be part of your team operating principles (discussed later in this chapter) on giving everyone the equal opportunity to verbally participate. For virtual teams, the object can be something shown on the screen during your video conference calls. At the next opportunity when you experience a team member using too much airtime, give the talking spoon technique a try. As project managers, team members, and stakeholders, we need to be able to articulate our point *and* let others express theirs.

Avoid Using Technology as a Crutch

Too often, people hide behind the keyboard rather than have conversations. They prefer to send an e-mail or text instead of engaging in a rich, interactive dialogue with another person or group. In having real-time conversations, you might gain valuable information, share new ideas, build relationships, and earn trust. However, meaningful interactions like these take time and effort. The use of technology "encourages us to act as if speed and convenience are the most important criteria for how we communicate."[5] But they are not! Remember that every interaction is important. Step out from behind the keyboard and take advantage of opportunities to have meaningful interactions—either in person or virtually. We will discuss more on the use of synchronous (real-time) and asynchronous communication tools in Chapter 7.

Be Present

With so much happening in today's dynamic project and working environments, it is easy to be distracted. Our minds are elsewhere. We are constantly interrupted by technology—phone, e-mails, text messages.

When we attend project meetings or have project conversations, it is possible that our mind is thinking about other tasks we need to get done. We might even be checking e-mail on our phones while another team member is speaking during a meeting. While we might be physically present, we are not mentally present. The project team needs you (and your mind) at your best on the topic at hand. It needs your active contribution and valuable ideas. Therefore, you need to be "there"—to be present—in every communication, conversation, and interaction.

Define Roles on the Team

For effective project communication, roles and responsibilities on the project need to be clearly defined. This should be done at the project kick-off meeting. To accelerate the process of establishing role definitions, start with roles that have been previously defined in other projects, for example, the project manager, project coordinator, team member, project sponsor, functional manager, etc. At the project kick-off meeting, review the sample roles together. Make adjustments specific to this project and this project team. Make sure that responsibilities for project communication are clearly defined for each role. Once the roles and responsibilities have been established and agreed upon, put the role definitions into your project plan. Everyone should refer to them as needed throughout the project.

Lead by Example

John Wooden, legendary American basketball player and coach, once said, "The most powerful leadership tool you have is your personal example."[6] As a participant on the project team, you should be role modeling what you consider to be good communication practices and acceptable behaviors. If you set good communication examples and actions, psychology indicates that others will follow. It starts with you![7]

Avoid Silence

When project team members and stakeholders are not communicating, there is a risk that these groups will start having conversations among themselves. This can create a foundation for even bigger problems, misunderstandings, and potential conflict. A quick "check-in" is better than saying nothing at all. In some company cultures or project teams, silence means acceptance. In other words, if you do not respond, you are agreeing to the decision, action, or content.

Use the Rule of Seven

The origin of the rule of seven started in marketing, where buyers needed to see and hear the same message seven different ways before they would make a purchase. The same concept can be applied to project communication. Aim to repeat the same message seven times, in seven different ways, to ensure everyone understands and receives the same message. What does the rule of seven look like in a project? Here is an example.

Susie is the project manager. She has created a lessons learned document in the electronic project folder. At each status meeting, Susie communicates that no one has posted information in the lessons learned folder and asks everyone to write their lessons learned. At the next team meeting, the lessons learned document (or log) is still empty. To set the example, Susie starts posting information in the lessons learned log and communicates that she has done so. She tries the rule of seven approach, using seven different ways to remind the team to take action. She uses a combination of formal and informal communication, as well as a mix of verbal and written communication. We'll talk more about formal and informal communication later in this chapter.

1. Susie clearly states the reminder at each status meeting.
2. She includes a lessons learned category in status reports.
3. Susie adds a reminder in her e-mail signature.
4. She posts her own lessons learned each week, then shares the updates with each team member via e-mail.
5. Susie asks each member of the project team to share two lessons learned at the weekly stand-up meeting—one positive result and one negative result.

6. She sets up checkpoints throughout the project to capture lessons learned.

7. Susie creates and shares a short video about lessons learned with the project team.

As a result, she sees that each member of her project team is now actively participating in capturing lessons learned on the project. The rule of seven really does work! Consider doing a similar activity: Try delivering the same message in seven different ways and see the difference. Then share the results with your project team.

Use Push, Pull, and Interactive Methods

On a project, there are numerous communication methods that the project team will use. Push communication methods require that the information be sent out. Pull communication methods require individuals to come to where the information is located, whether that location is physical or virtual. Interactive communication methods use an exchange of information. In their book *Contemporary Project Management*, Timothy Kloppenborg, Vittal Anantatmula, and Kathryn Wells provide examples of each method (Table 4.1).

Table 4.1 Examples of push, pull, and interactive communication methods[8]

Push methods	Pull methods	Interactive methods
Instant messaging	Shared document	Phone call
E-mail	repositories	Teleconference
Voicemail	Intranet	Wikis
Text	Blog (repository)	VOIP/videoconferencing
Project reports	Bulletin boards	Groupware
Presentations	Kanban boards	Meetings

Utilize Training

Project management is both about knowledge (training) and experience. To qualify for many project management certifications, both project education hours and project experience hours may be required. Most project professionals have taken classes and studied project management. However, how much training have we done to learn about communicating? If 90 percent of a project manager's time is spent communicating, can we be really good at it just by experience? Probably not. Consider taking some communication classes. Read books on project communication—including this one! Follow blogs to learn more about effective communication. If you do not know where to begin, refer to Appendix B for a list of books and other resources.

Be a Continuous Learner

Look for opportunities to grow your communication skills, knowledge, and experience. Dr. Donald Clifton, psychologist, educator, and developer of the CliftonStrengths® assessment, said, "To produce excellence, you must study excellence."[9] Start doing both today—studying *and* producing project communication excellence.

Implement Team Operating Principles

Team operating principles (or ground rules) outline the way communication is handled, what to expect, and who is responsible, along with many other aspects of working together. Some people call it a "team contract" or "team agreement." Regardless of what it is called, it shows formally that all team members have made a commitment on how they will work together—including communication protocols and expectations.

Too often on a project team, we hear, "What are you expecting from me?" During the project kick-off meeting, make sure that expectations are set, aligned, and agreed upon as individuals and as a team. Establishing expectations can be a mechanism to reduce uncertainty for team members and reduce risk in the project by providing clarity for stakeholders. Setting clear expectations is essential and should be documented in the team operating principles and role definitions.

A list of sample ground rules can be found in Appendix E. Exhibit 4.1 highlights some ground rules specifically for communication protocols and setting expectations.

Exhibit 4.1

Sample ground rules for team communications

- The project manager will send a status update every Friday via e-mail by 5:00 p.m.
- Team leaders are responsible for updating any tasks that are impacted by the status update no later than 9:00 a.m. on Monday morning.
- Team members should talk with a team lead for clarification about tasks.
- The project sponsor is responsible for updating the leadership team on the project's status at least once a month or as requested.
- Inquiries about the status of the project that come in to any member of the team should be reported to the project manager.
- The project team will have at least one monthly face-to-face meeting or teleconference for an internal status update. All team members are expected to attend and participate in the meeting.
- All meeting invitations must include an agenda or description of the purpose of the meeting and the expected outcomes.
- No cell phones are to be used in project meetings; laptops should only be used for notetaking or other actions relevant to the meeting (no checking e-mail).
- If you are making a task or assignment, provide a clear, specific deadline of when you need it.
- Keep e-mail threads on topic. If you need to discuss a new topic, send a new e-mail rather than a reply.

To be most effective, ground rules should be established together as a team. This ensures everyone participates in creating the ground rules and has an opportunity to ask questions for increased clarity; it also creates greater buy-in so that the ground rules are more likely to be used and followed. Ground rules should be revisited regularly (more frequently in the beginning of the project) to ensure that communications are being executed effectively both inside and outside the project team. Another benefit of setting initial guidelines around communication is that they can divert the target of individuals' displeasure from other people to the process, which can depersonalize communication breakdowns and avoid conflict. We will talk more about conflict in Chapter 9.

Your team's operating principles will probably look different from Exhibit 4.1. The key is (1) to have them, (2) to create them as a group, and (3) to use them.

Team ground rules:

1. Have them.
2. Create them as a group.
3. Use them.

Use Inclusive Language—No Jargon

Many professions have their own terminology and word usage to talk about what they do and how they do it. You may have experienced this when talking with someone from another area of expertise, and had difficulty understanding the technical language they used to describe a function of their work. Project management has its own language as well, and you should be cautious about using that language with stakeholders— both inside and outside the project team—who are not project managers or experienced project professionals. Use words and expressions that are inclusive of all individuals and groups. Jargon and technical language can exclude others, which can create uncertainty, misunderstanding, and conflict.

As noted in Chapter 1, the call to communicate "in the project language" was removed in the very first revision of the *PMBOK® Guide*. In PMI's "The High Cost of Low Performance: The Essential Role of Communications" report, one of the biggest problem areas in project communication stems from "challenges surrounding the language used to deliver project-related information, which is often unclear and peppered with project management jargon."[10] When projects are communicated "in the language of the audience,"[11] the project is more likely to succeed. Knowing your audience (see Chapter 3) helps you know the language to use when communicating about the project. In general, however, a good rule is to limit project management jargon to only those on the project team whom you are certain will understand the language.

You may want to adjust the language you use when communicating with different levels in the organization as well, based upon their interests. For example:

- When communicating with **executives and senior management**, their interest may be the bottom-line impact and a high-level summary of the project.
- When communicating with **functional managers**, their interest may be in the people and resources, specifically the team members they have assigned to work on the project.
- When communicating with **outside stakeholders**, their interest may be in progress, status updates, and results achieved.
- When communicating with the **project team,** their interest may be staying on schedule, completing tasks, addressing risks, and delivering project success.

Whatever their interest, know your audience and adjust your communication to be inclusive of who they are and what their stakes are in the project (see Chapter 3).

Formal and Informal Communication

As we work and communicate with different levels in the organization, we also use different communication methods. You can categorize most project communications into four types: formal written, informal written, formal verbal, and informal verbal[12] (Figure 4.1). What are examples of each type?

- Formal written—When you are documenting a project problem, signing a vendor contract, or preparing documentation for your project (project charter, status reports, etc.), this is formal written communication. Typically, formal written communication requires planning or preparing.

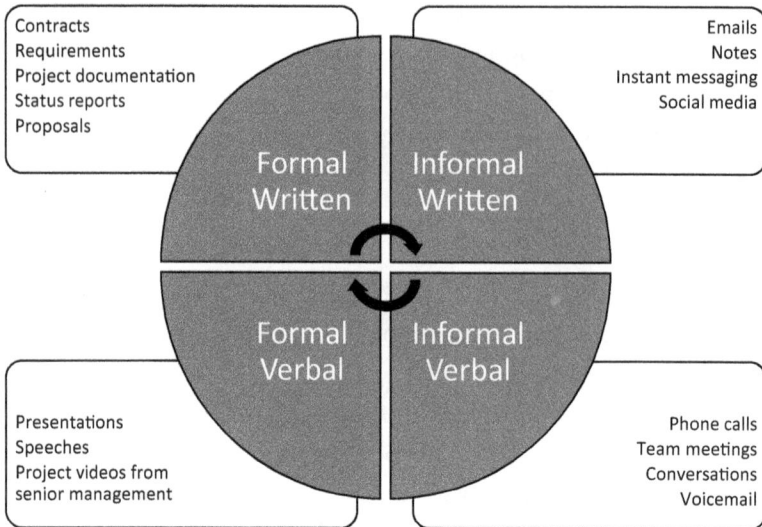

Figure 4.1 Types of formal and informal communication

- Informal written—When you send an e-mail or text message, or hand a note to someone about the project, this is a type of informal written communication.
- Formal verbal—When you give a speech or deliver a presentation with project updates, this is formal verbal communication. Again, there is an element of planning or preparation.
- Informal verbal—When you are chatting with your colleagues about the project, or meeting for coffee to discuss project tasks, this is a type of informal verbal communication.

Choose the right type of communication based on the outcome(s) you are trying to achieve. Be cautious when using informal communication where action or documentation is needed. For example, you have a spontaneous conversation with another project team member and say, "Oh, can you please take care of that?" Then nothing happens. There is no follow-up because it is not documented. In project management, if it is not documented, it didn't happen!

In project management, if it is not documented, it didn't happen!

Scaling Communications for Project Size

When communicating, the size and complexity of the project will impact your communication. A small project may have more informal communication than a large project. A colocated project team where everyone sits together may have more flexibility in communicating, since it is easier to walk over and talk with another team member face-to-face. On regulatory projects, you may have more formal communication—written and verbal—than on nonregulatory projects. Regardless of the project size or type, we need to scale our communications to fit.

What does "communication scaling" mean? Like many aspects of project management, it depends on the project. Here are some considerations as you scale your communications for the project at hand.

Communication scaling can pertain to the *amount of communication or information shared*. Depending on the complexity and priority of the project, you may only need to communicate status updates on a weekly basis, or you may need to provide in-depth progress reports to some individuals or groups on a near-daily basis. Senior executives tend to like "at-a-glance" communication methods like dashboards. A dashboard provides only high-level information, similar to an executive summary. Then the executive can ask for more details if desired. (As project managers, we need to be ready to communicate the details at all times!) Effective project managers scale their communication to create the "dashboard" effect—with communications that provide high-level overviews of what is happening on the project, as well as detailed background information ready when stakeholders need it. (We will talk more about dashboards as a communication tool in Chapter 7.)

Communication scaling can pertain to the *impact of miscommunication*. When we have one-on-one or interpersonal communication, there is no scaling. Any miscommunicated information initially stays between the two parties and can be clarified more easily, especially when corrected as soon as possible. However, if we send the wrong message to a large group of stakeholders, your poor communication can scale exponentially. You can cause difficulties with a larger group of stakeholders; this makes the problem harder to correct, and also opens the door to further damage as those stakeholders discuss it with even more people and further amplify the damage caused by the poor communication.

Communication scaling can pertain to the *different types of groups.* Different organizations involved in the project will require communications specific to their role. Public stakeholder groups who do not participate in but are affected by a project (for example, community members impacted by a construction project) will need separate communications that address their interests in the project. See Chapter 3 for more about understanding your audience.

Communication scaling can pertain to the *number of people involved.* Small projects may require relatively few communication methods, especially if there are only a few team members or external stakeholders. Large projects will require you to scale your communications using many different methods for many different audiences, such as multiple organizations participating in the project and multiple stakeholder groups.

Communication scaling can pertain to *tools.* You can build efficiencies into your project communications by utilizing the tools which best serve your different audiences. The project team, for example, might function most efficiently when using a cloud-based team collaboration tool. An Internet site might work best when there is a large project with many stakeholders, offering extensive information that multiple groups need to access. (See Chapter 7 for more about choosing communication tools.)

Communication scaling can pertain to the *diversity of the audience.* You may need to add more methods of communication or more frequent communication to your plan to accommodate the information needs of diverse stakeholders. It is essential to get regular feedback to make sure that your message is delivered and clearly understood. (See Chapter 6 for more information on feedback.)

Putting It into Practice

Here are a few practical tips, fun activities, and useful ideas for how you can implement the concepts in this chapter into your project environment. Note that ideas listed in one type of team may be adapted to other teams. Be creative. Use these as a starting point. Add your own ideas to build your communications toolkit.

Starting with the basics	
Traditional project teams	• Set the example: Demonstrate good project communication behaviors you expect from other team members. • Put a "jargon jar" in your team room. Every time a team member uses project management jargon with an outside stakeholder, they must contribute a small amount of money to the jar. At the end of the project or at a project milestone, use the money in the jar to buy the team a treat, such as coffee, lunch, or gift cards (depending on how much money is in the jar). • Try the talking spoon exercise in your team meetings. Only the person holding the spoon (or any other object you can hold, such as a marker) can speak. When that person is finished, they put down the spoon and then another person can pick it up and speak.
Agile project teams	• As a team, create ground rules for your stand-up meetings so that everyone is on board with the process. • Make sure each meeting has a facilitator to keep the conversation on track. Ask a different team member to serve as facilitator for each meeting so they can gain valuable experience. • For those who have an interest in your project, invite them to attend sprint reviews. This will show the team "in action" and validate the work that has been completed. Over time, it will strengthen trust and relationships, and reduce stakeholder uncertainty.
Virtual project teams	• Have each member of the team share what they think it means to be a "high-performing project team." • Choose a unique term that you might use in your project, such as "virtual roundtable." Have each member of the team share how they interpret that term. • Look for opportunities to use both formal and informal communication.

Summary

Whether you are communicating on a project, or communicating in general, it is important to start with the basics. Use practical techniques and sensible approaches for effectively delivering your message. Research has shown that high-performing teams and organizations are better at communicating key project concepts, delivering their messages in a timely manner using inclusive language and the right methods, and effectively using formal project communications management plans. With the increase in the number of different ways to communicate, there are many things to consider in your project communications.

Scaling your project communications pertains to the amount of communication shared, the impact of the communication, the size and types of stakeholder groups, the various tools, and the diversity of the audience. And don't forget that words matter. Regardless of how they are delivered—formal, informal, written, or verbal—words have a lasting impact!

Key Questions

1. Review the "Things to Consider" section at the beginning of this chapter. What would you add from your own experiences when communicating on projects?

2. In your next communication interaction or project team meeting, intentionally put the six active listening skills listed in this chapter to use.

3. Try delivering the same message in seven different ways and see the difference. Then share the results with your project team.

Notes

1. Toastmasters International (2019), accessed September 23, 2019, https://www.toastmasters.org/magazine/magazine-issues/2019/sep/inspiring-quotes-for-leaders.
2. Project Management Institute (2013), p. 6.
3. Center for Creative Leadership, https://www.ccl.org/articles/leading-effectively-articles/coaching-others-use-active-listening-skills/.
4. Bill Gates, https://www.azquotes.com/author/5382-Bill_Gates/tag/feedback.
5. Tumlin (2013), p. 22.
6. Wooden, https://www.azquotes.com/quote/866260.
7. Tumlin (2013), p. 34.
8. Kloppenborg, et al. (2019), p. 190.
9. Clifton and Anderson (2006), p. xv.

10. Project Management Institute (2013), p. 4.

11. Project Management Institute (2013), p. 5.

12. Burke and Barron (2014), p. 292.

References

Bill Gates. 2019. https://www.azquotes.com/author/5382-Bill_Gates/tag /feedback, (accessed May 30, 2019).

Burke, R. and S. Barron. 2014. *Project Management Leadership: Building Creative Teams.* West Sussex, UK: John Wiley & Sons, Ltd.

Center for Creative Leadership. 2019. "Use Active Listening to Coach Others." https://www.ccl.org/articles/leading-effectively-articles/coaching-others -use-active-listening-skills/, (accessed August 5, 2019).

Center for Creative Leadership and M. H. Hoppe. 2006. *Active Listening: Improve Your Ability to Listen and Lead.* Greensboro, NC: Center for Creative Leadership.

Clifton, D. O., E. Anderson, and L. A. Schreiner. 2006. *StrengthsQuest: Discover and Develop Your Strengths in Academic, Career, and Beyond.* New York, NY: Gallup Press.

Kloppenborg, T. J., V. Anantatmula, and K. N. Wells. 2019. *Contemporary Project Management,* 4th ed. Stamford, CT: Cengage Learning.

Project Management Institute. 2013. "The High Cost of Low Performance: The Essential Role of Communications." Newtown Square, PA: Project Management Institute.

Toastmasters International. September, 2019. "Inspiring Quotes for Leaders." https://www.toastmasters.org/magazine/magazine-issues/2019/ sep/inspiring-quotes-for-leaders, (accessed September 23, 2019).

Tumlin, G. 2013. *Stop Talking, Start Communicating.* New York, NY: McGraw-Hill Education.

Wooden, J. 2019. https://www.azquotes.com/quote/866260, (accessed August 8, 2019).

CHAPTER 5

Planning Project Communications

If you fail to prepare, you are preparing to fail.[1]
— The Reverend H. K. Williams, religious leader and author

Most often, we associate the concept of failing to plan or prepare with the overall project. If we fail to plan the project, we are planning for the project to fail. However, it can also be applied to planning communication on a project. What are the chances of project success if we fail to plan our communications? This chapter incorporates key concepts from other chapters in this book into the first process in the *PMBOK® Guide's* Project Communications Management Knowledge Area, which is Plan Communications Management (Figure 5.1).

The purpose of this chapter is to help you:

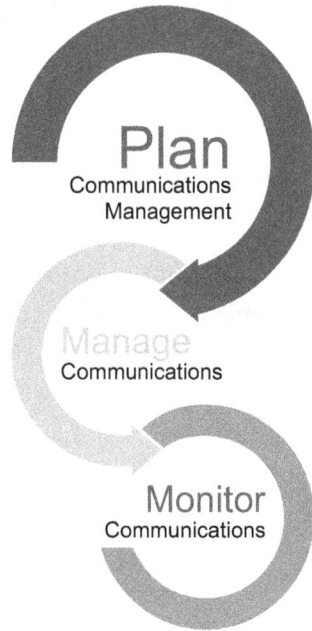

Figure 5.1 Plan communications

- Understand the purpose, content, and development of a project communications management plan

- Demonstrate how to effectively use a project communications management plan
- Examine a communications matrix
- Put it into practice: Planning communications in traditional, agile, and virtual project teams

As we work with, and communicate with, various stakeholder groups, having an effective project communications management plan is critical—not only to have it, but to use it! So, let's start with a question.

If you are a project manager, how much time do *you* spend communicating when working on a project? This refers to how much time you *are* spending communicating on a project, not how much time you *should* be spending. For team members, think about how much time you think your project manager spends communicating on a project. Put an X somewhere between 0 percent and 100 percent on the continuum below:

0%										100%	

According to the *PMBOK® Guide*, studies show that "top project managers spend about 90 percent of their time on a project in communicating"[2]—with external stakeholders, groups, project teams, individuals, management, project sponsor, and others. Hopefully, you marked your X near 90 percent!

To help you keep track of how much time you spend communicating, consider making a time log. For one or two days on a project, track how much of your time is spent communicating. Is it aligned with how much time you *think* you should be communicating? The results could be very enlightening. To get started, a daily log template can be found in Appendix C.

Since project managers are to be spending the majority of their time communicating, it is best to have a plan. A project communications management plan.

Project Communications Management Plan

The *PMBOK® Guide* defines Plan Communications Management as "the process for developing an appropriate approach and plan for project communications activities based on the information needs of each stake-holder or group, available organizational assets, and the needs of the project."[3] In other words, consider it your "how to" document. How will you communicate with various stakeholder groups? How will you utilize the processes, procedures, policies, plans, and knowledge already established by the organization? What new processes or procedures might be needed? What, when, and who will send and receive information—and how will that information be distributed? Where will project information be stored and how will it be retrieved? How will the information be disposed of at the end of the project? The purpose of a project communications management plan is to answer these and other questions in guiding the project team's communications to "ensure timely and appropriate planning, collection, creation, description, storage, retrieval, management, control, monitoring, and ultimate disposition of project information."[4]

Plan Communications Management happens in the *planning* process group. It is our "communications road map." It is our guide for keeping everyone informed—with the right message, at the right time, using the right methods, for the right reasons. The other chapters in this book provide insight into these different factors. The project communications management plan is where you bring them all together.

There are many forms of a project communications management plan. As with any project management tool, technique, or template, you may need to tailor it to fit your project and organization. More complex, larger projects will have a very comprehensive project communications management plan. A comprehensive project communications management plan may include items like your communications approach or strategy, roles and responsibilities, change control, organizational policies and procedures, meeting rules, technology considerations, templates, and other pertinent content. For a small project, the project communications management plan may simply have one or two items.

Regardless of the size or complexity of the project, here is a word of caution: Just because you have a template or form does not mean that you fill it out and you are done. Project management is not about "form filling." It is about adapting the templates, tools, and techniques to meet your project, stakeholder, and organizational needs—and then using them!

Project management is not about "form filling." It is about adapting the templates, tools, and techniques to meet your project, stakeholder, and organizational needs—and then using them!

Take a look at the example in Exhibit 5.1. This is a sample outline of a table of contents for a project communications management plan. You can find more detail about the individual elements of this sample outline in Appendix C.

Exhibit 5.1

Communications management plan table of contents—sample outline

Table of contents

1. Overview and Purpose
2. Organizational Policies and Procedures
   a. Communications Processes
   b. Technology and Information Storage
3. Stakeholder Communications
4. Communications Matrix
5. Change Control
6. Project Team
   a. Contact Information
   b. Roles and Responsibilities
   c. Reports
   d. Meetings and Calls
7. Signatures
8. Appendix 1: Glossary of Terms/Abbreviations
9. Appendix 2: Communication Templates
10. Appendix 3: Communication Examples
11. Version Control

Adding a glossary with a list of terminology and abbreviations that are pertinent to your project, organization, or industry helps to avoid misunderstandings, especially on global, culturally diverse project teams.

Attaching documents such as diagrams, charts, templates, and communication examples helps facilitate the sharing of project information. Depending on the size and complexity of your project, your table of contents may look different and contain more or fewer elements than the sample outline in Exhibit 5.1.

One additional recommendation: Do not make your project communications management plan so voluminous and so complicated that no one uses it. It needs to be proportionate to the size and complexity of your project, and the project experience of your team. The less project management experience your team has, the more information is included in your project communications management plan. Otherwise, there is a greater risk of miscommunication occurring.

Your project communications management plan must be crystal clear. It needs to provide guidance to the project team, to avoid any ambiguity or uncertainty in project communications logistics and fundamentals. It is also an evolving "how to" document throughout the life of the project. As communication challenges arise, update your project communications management plan so that future challenges can be quickly addressed or avoided.

Create the Plan. Follow the Plan.

When developing a project communications management plan, where do you begin? Start by reviewing the project communications management plans of previous, similar projects. Review the lessons learned. What worked well? What needed improvement? What project communications areas were challenging? Share and discuss the findings with your project team. You can learn a lot from the experiences of other project teams and avoid mistakes that others have made. Once you have completed the review and discussion, you can start to collaborate and develop your own project communications management plan as a team. Working as a team will ensure that the collective thoughts, ideas, and resources from the team are being considered and incorporated. In addition to team building, working together adds greater experience and value to your plan, which benefits the team and stakeholders.

Your project communications management plan should include all stakeholders that you have identified in your project (see Chapter 3), and address the aspects of the project that impact them most. Incorporate the basics of good project communication discussed in Chapter 4, and make sure your plan aligns with the ground rules you set with your team (see Appendix E). The information in Chapter 7 will help you choose the best tools for executing your plan. Since all projects bring about change, your project communications management plan should incorporate elements for handling and communicating that change with stakeholders, as presented in Chapter 8. The content in Chapter 9 will assist you in handling conflict when it occurs, both when working together as a team and when working with outside stakeholders.

The project communications management plan is designed to be developed by, and used by, the project team to ensure that stakeholders are receiving the project information that they need, and that the project communications are effective. The project communications management plan is *one* element in the overall project plan. You may have other "management plans" for scope, schedule, cost, quality, resources, risks, procurement, and/or stakeholders. Therefore, you will probably not be sharing your project communications management plan with those outside the team, unless you are sharing the entire project plan.

Once the project communications management plan has been developed, you now need to follow it. Here is a partial list of techniques to ensure your project communications are being used effectively.

1. **Take ownership**: In project management, ownership is everything. Make sure that someone on the team owns the project communications management plan. This individual is responsible for ensuring that the project communications management plan gets followed properly, reviewed regularly, and updated as needed.
2. **Review regularly**: Key elements in the project communications management plan should be reviewed at every project status meeting. Important communications should be reflected in project status reports.
3. **Keep a log**: With so much information being shared on a project, maintain a log (or journal) of critical communications. This will serve you well when documenting lessons learned.
4. **Get feedback**: Getting feedback is essential for effective project communications. In communicating and engaging with stakeholders, listen to their feedback and incorporate relevant input. We will discuss feedback further in Chapter 6.

5. **Do a systems assessment**: Ask the project team and others who are accessing project information if systems for storing and retrieving project information are working properly. Make necessary adjustments or provide ongoing assistance.

6. **Ask questions**: If you are uncertain about a process in the project communications management plan or a specific message, ask others. Get clarity before sending project information. One valuable technique is to have others read (or listen to) your message before sending (or saying) it. Ask: How does this read to you? How does this sound to you? This activity can make a tremendous difference.

7. **Lead by example**: Make sure that you are effectively communicating. Over time, others will see your example and aspire to do the same.

8. **Make updates**: If something is not working in your project communications, make changes. As changes occur, make necessary updates to the project communications management plan. Keep track of changes through proper revision control. Remember, the project communications management plan evolves over the life of the project.

As you gain more project communications experience, add to this list. Keep it handy as an easy reference to ensure that you are building these actions into your project communications.

Having a project communications management plan means using it. However, don't overlook the informal communications that often take place on a project. For example, osmotic communications—a term coined by Alistair Cockburn, coauthor of the Agile Manifesto—occur when team members pick up relevant information through the conversations of other team members seated in the same room. These informal discussions and interactions happen outside your project communications management plan, and may also need to be documented.

Project Communications Take Time

How does a project manager balance communicating with getting the work done on a project, especially if project managers truly do spend 90 percent of their time communicating? The answer: it depends. It depends on the size and complexity of the project. For example, if the size of the project is micro or small, the project manager will do more project work, and less project managing. The communication time will be less on a micro or small project because there are fewer deliverables, the timeline is shorter, and the team is smaller. However, for medium, large, or superlarge projects which are highly complex, lengthy, and may have a large project team and many stakeholders, the project manager will spend more time communicating, and less time actually doing project work on deliverables and tasks.

For these types of projects (large, complex, lengthy), project teams may consider adding a person to the project team who is an expert in communication. Often, you will have subject matter experts in various fields—technology, finance, engineering, marketing, etc.—on the project team. Having a communication expert on the project team could be extremely beneficial. This individual would work closely with the project manager to help orchestrate and support communications, assist in creating and executing the project communications management plan, and help reduce the risk of the wrong message being sent to the wrong stakeholder groups, at the wrong time, for the wrong purpose. Keep in mind, however, that it is the project manager who is ultimately responsible for ensuring that the project communications management plan is created and properly executed.

While the project manager is usually the "outward-facing voice" on the project, it is the responsibility of all project team members to communicate—and to be skillful communicators. (Chapters 4 and 7 provide more information for the entire project team on effective communication approaches and tools.) Effective communication skills enable the team to provide clarity, reduce uncertainty, meet stakeholder expectations, demonstrate accountability, and build trust. Make sure the team is also utilizing the team operating principles to help guide their communications as outlined in Chapter 4.

Communications Matrix

A communications matrix provides an "at a glance" document to quickly assess what information needs to be distributed, to whom, when, and how. A communications matrix can also take many forms and is developed together by the project team. Information that is included in a communications matrix can come from a variety of sources—the sponsor, project manager, management, project team, stakeholder analysis, lessons learned from other projects, company requirements, etc. Table 5.1 shows an example of a project communications matrix.

Table 5.1 Project communications matrix example

Communication	Format	Timing	Owner	Recipients	Comments
Status reports	E-mail	Weekly	Project manager	Project team and sponsor	Use one-page status report template
Status meetings	In-person or virtual/ conference call	Weekly	Project manager	Project team	30 minutes or less; distribute status report in advance
Status meeting minutes	E-mail	Within 24 hours of status meeting	Project coordinator	Project team	Includes action items and decisions
Action items	E-mail	As needed	Project coordinator	Project team	Each action item has follow-up due date and will be reviewed at each status meeting
Budget reports	E-mail and in-person review	Monthly	Project manager	Project team, sponsor, key management personnel	Use budget report template
Schedule updates	E-mail and in-person review	Monthly	Project manager	Project team, sponsor	Provide summary of schedule updates to key management
Risk review	In-person or virtual/ conference call	Weekly	Project manager	Project team, sponsor	Include in weekly status meetings
Issues or problem log	E-mail	As needed	Project manager	Project team, sponsor	Include in weekly status meetings

For other documents, determine the format, timing, audience, and other considerations based on the urgency, sensitivity, project needs, and stakeholder expectations.

Since projects have lots of information, having an electronic document repository can be helpful. This is a secure online location where all project data can be stored. Instead of e-mailing documents, a link to the information can be provided. This helps with accessibility, version control, and data security.

Putting It into Practice

Here are a few practical tips, fun activities, and useful ideas for how you can implement the concepts in this chapter into your project environment. Note that ideas listed in one type of team may be adapted to other teams. Be creative. Use these as a starting point. Add your own ideas to build your communications toolkit.

Planning project communications	
Traditional project teams	• Do a team survey to gather information on communication styles, communication preferences, technology challenges, experiences, etc. • Establish roles and responsibilities for each participant on the project—project manager, project coordinator, sponsor, team member, subject matter expert, etc.—specifically focused on communicating and setting expectations. Review these roles and responsibilities at the project kick-off meeting. • Look for opportunities where you can meet face-to-face with key stakeholders. Share how you plan to communicate with them, and answer their questions. This will help build relationships, so that when something happens, you have an existing relationship as a foundation.
Agile project teams	• Ensure that the team is using proper agile communication methods for communicating frequently and effectively—and quickly. One way agile teams do this is to use information radiators or Big Visible Charts, which provide a highly visible way to convey project information at a glance. • Plan out a communication calendar and post it in your team room or project team site. List the planned communication activities scheduled for each day. Visually "check off" activities as they are completed, and report on this progress at least weekly with the project team. • If the team is new to agile concepts, plan and conduct training opportunities where team members can experiment with agile concepts (including communicating using artifacts and meetings).

Virtual project teams	• Create a glossary of terms together so that team members in different cultures have a clear understanding of the terms that will be used on the project. • When conducting virtual meetings and conference calls, be respectful of the different time zones for team members. Plan to rotate the meeting times to minimize the inconvenience of early-morning or late-night conference calls. • In planning communication with virtual teams, make sure you have a backup plan established. This might be when technology fails, when communication breaks down, when a conflict occurs, or when an emergency happens. Plan out the "what if's" so that when they occur, your virtual team is ready.

Summary

Project communication is essential to project success. A project communications management plan helps you and the project team stay on track in keeping others informed—with the right message, at the right time, for the right purpose. As the project team implements the project communications management plan, the team may find adjustments need to be made. The project communications management plan should evolve throughout the life of the project. There are several techniques that you can use to ensure that your project communications management plan is being used effectively. Consider adding a communications specialist to your project team when needed.

Project communications take time. A communications matrix provides an "at a glance" look at project communications. And finally: If you fail to plan your project communications, you plan to fail. Don't overlook the importance and value of having an effective project communications management plan for your project—not only to have it, but to use it!

Key Questions

1. Create a time log for tracking your project communications. For 1 or 2 days, track how much time you spend communicating on the project. Review the results. What surprised you? What didn't surprise you?

2. What challenges or project risks might you encounter if your project team does not have a project communications management plan?

3. Take a look at the list of techniques presented in this chapter to ensure your project communications management plan is being used effectively. What other techniques would you add to the list and why?

Notes

1. Williams (1919), p. 81.
2. Project Management Institute (2017), *PMBOK® Guide*, 6th ed., p. 61.
3. Project Management Institute (2017), *PMBOK® Guide*, 6th ed., p. 359.
4. Kloppenborg et al. (2015), pp. 443–444.

References

Kloppenborg, T. J., V. Anantatmula, K. N. Wells. 2015. *Contemporary Project Management,* 3rd ed. Stamford, CT: Cengage Learning.

Project Management Institute. 2017. *A Guide to the Project Management Body of Knowledge.* 6th ed. Newtown Square, PA: Project Management Institute.

Williams, H. K. 1919. "Young People's Service." *The Biblical World,* 53, no 1, pp. 80–81. The University of Chicago Press: Chicago, Illinois.

CHAPTER 6

Managing and Monitoring Project Communications

The great enemy of communication, we find, is the illusion of it.[1]
—William H. Whyte, journalist and author

Now that you have planned your project communications, what's next? To properly manage and carefully monitor your project communications! This chapter focuses on the next two processes in the *PMBOK® Guide*: managing and monitoring project communications. We will be looking at these areas through the lens of content presented throughout the book (Figure 6.1).

The purpose of this chapter is to help you:

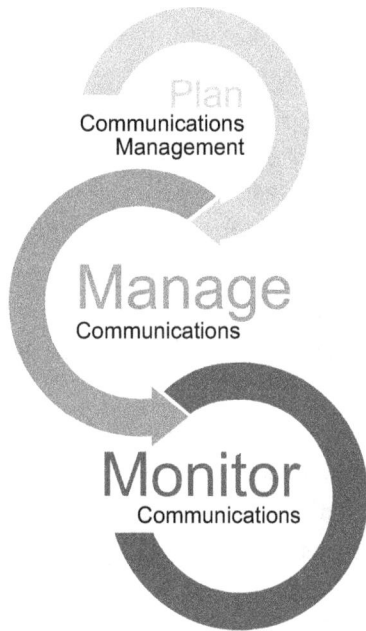

Figure 6.1 Manage and monitor communications

- Build key skills needed to address stakeholders' practical needs and personal needs when communicating on projects—including a five-step approach
- Measure the effectiveness of your project communications
- Understand the importance of incorporating feedback loops

- Examine lessons learned and retrospectives
- Put it into practice: Managing and monitoring communications in traditional, agile, and virtual project teams

Managing communications happens in the *executing* process group. This is when work is being done on the project. This is also the time when the project team is following their project communications management plan outlined in Chapter 5. Per the definition in the *PMBOK® Guide*, managing communications is "the process of ensuring timely and appropriate collection, creation, distribution, storage, retrieval, management, monitoring, and the ultimate disposition of project information."[2]

Why is this important? Among the project team, we need to make sure that everyone who is working on the project is kept informed—that they have the information they need for successful completion of their assigned tasks and deliverables. Outside the project team, we need to ensure that stakeholders are also well informed—that they have the information they need to stay up-to-date and continue to support the project, or move from being unaware or resisting the project to a more supportive position (see Chapter 3).

Monitoring communications occurs in the *monitoring and controlling* process group. In earlier versions of the *PMBOK® Guide* (see Chapter 1), this process contained monitor *and control* communications. In the sixth edition of the *PMBOK® Guide*, the Control Communications process was eliminated since there are many things outside the purview of the project team that they cannot control, such as when, how, where, or why people communicate.[3] However, there are still some elements of control in communicating on projects. While we may not be able to control everything—like when and how stakeholders communicate—we *can* control our reaction, attitude, approach, and response to their communications.

During monitoring communications, providing continuous oversight is necessary to constantly be aware of the communication taking place throughout the project, whether it is communicating about project status, activities, or results, or keeping stakeholders current with project information.

Over the life of the project, we should also seek opportunities to make improvements in our communications, processes, and environment. This can be done through feedback, surveys, ongoing conversations, etc.—various ways where we are asking for (and using) the valuable inputs and diverse perspectives of others. As the *PMBOK® Guide* clearly states, your project communications management plan should be revisited regularly and revised as needed.[4] When the team receives input on implementing more effective ways of communicating with stakeholders, the project communications management plan should be updated to reflect this improved way of working.

And finally, we need to deliver project information in a way that influences and inspires, that reduces uncertainty and builds trust, and that grows the project knowledge and support of individuals and groups interested in our project at all levels, both inside and outside the organization.

Managing Project Communications

From a broad perspective, managing communications on a project means ensuring that the project communications management plan is being executed. In practice, managing communications starts with managing your conversations with all stakeholders. Ideally, your interactions end by accomplishing at least one of the following:

- Providing information needed to support the role of the person/group or their project needs
- Reducing their uncertainty about the project, their role, or others involved in the project
- Building their trust in the project's goals, plan, and participants

So how do you effectively manage conversations? Let's look at the conversation process developed by Development Dimensions International (DDI). DDI is a global leadership consulting firm that helps organizations hire, promote, and develop exceptional leaders. From first-time managers to C-suite executives, DDI is by leaders' sides, supporting them in every critical moment of leadership. Built on five decades of research and experience in the science of leadership, DDI's evidence-based assessment and development solutions enable millions of leaders around the world to succeed, propelling their organizations to new heights. For more information, visit https://www.ddiworld.com/.

Through DDI's years of extensive study and research, they found that "people come to work with both practical needs (to get work done) and personal needs (to be respected and valued)."[5] The same is true with project teams. Team members are focused on getting the work done to achieve the project objective (practical needs) and to know that they are valued contributors and integral key members to the project team (personal needs). The skills used to meet the personal and practical needs in our communications are called "Interaction Essentials[SM]." Wouldn't it be wonderful if all project communications were addressing both the personal and practical needs of the project team and stakeholders?

Personal Needs

Let's start with managing project communications by addressing personal needs. This includes everyone inside and outside the project team who has an interest in our project. According to DDI, the five key principles are:

1. Self-esteem
2. Empathy
3. Involvement
4. Share
5. Support

Self-Esteem

By maintaining or enhancing self-esteem, we are managing communications by reassuring team members that they have the necessary expertise to be part of the team, by giving praise for doing a great job, or suggesting a better way of working.

To maintain self-esteem, we would have fact-based discussions (see Chapter 9), focus on the problem (not the person), and show our respect and support.

Example: "Joe, you have the most knowledge about the problem on this project. This project is very important to our customers. We really need your expertise in handling this situation."

To enhance self-esteem, we would focus on recognizing great ideas and key contributions. This is an opportunity to build and show confidence in the project team member or stakeholder. In order to do this, we must be specific and sincere.

Example: "Sally, great job in speaking up today at the project team meeting to express your concerns with the project schedule. You are correct. It is very aggressive. Thanks for pointing this out. I really appreciate your ongoing contributions to the team."

Empathy

By listening and responding with empathy, we are managing communications to build understanding, address the positive and negative emotions, and show that we care about others' feelings while working with the facts.

Example: "Brian, I know this is a very large, complex project. You might be feeling a bit overwhelmed with doing all this project work, as well as getting your regular work done."

Involvement

By asking for help and encouraging involvement, we are managing communications to seek ideas, ask for help, get commitment, and really be involved with the project and working together as a team. This is an opportunity to ask open-ended questions.

> *Example: "Maria, now that we have developed the project plan together, what are your thoughts? What does project success look like for you?"*

Share

By sharing our thoughts, feelings, and rationale, we are managing communications to build trust. *Trust is everything* when it comes to working as a high-performing project team. To build trust, we must share our feelings, have open and honest communications, and discuss "why" decisions, changes, or actions are taken. The benefit of sharing is building relationships.

> *Example: "I understand how you are feeling. I had a similar experience working on a large, complex project, and worried about getting my regular work done. By developing a simple time management system, I scheduled time in my calendar to do project work, and time for my operations work. It worked for me. It might also work for you."*

Support

By providing support without removing responsibility, we are managing communications to build ownership. In managing projects, everything is "owned" by someone. When you own a task or responsibility, you are more likely to see it to completion and be successful. As the project manager, it is your responsibility to provide the necessary resources to help team members get their project tasks done and remove any obstacles that get in their way. With support, you are building confidence in others to be successful.

> *Example: "What can I do to help you? What is in your way of getting the project done? Perhaps there are some barriers that I can remove for you to be successful."*

Using these five key principles—self-esteem, empathy, involvement, share, and support—in managing project communications ensures that the personal needs of your project team and stakeholders are being addressed. That they feel "valued, respected, and understood." How will you know their personal needs? For the project team, we suggest simply asking each team member. For outside stakeholders, we suggest identifying their needs during stakeholder analysis and documenting them in your stakeholder register as part of knowing your audience (see Chapter 3).

Practical Needs

Now let's look at the practical needs, which focus on a series of five steps. DDI's research has proven that in order to have effective communications and conversations, there needs to be a structure to address the practical needs of individuals and stakeholders. DDI provides a "five-step conversation roadmap" called the Interaction Guidelines. Consider it as "a vehicle to frame conversations in a quick, logical, and thorough way—from start to finish—to cover all the specific information people need" on the project.[6]

This approach can be used with any conversation or interaction—any time—with anyone associated with the project. To meet the practical needs and to ensure that you have addressed all items that need discussing, the five steps in the Interaction Guidelines provide an excellent framework to follow. So, what are the five steps? They are:

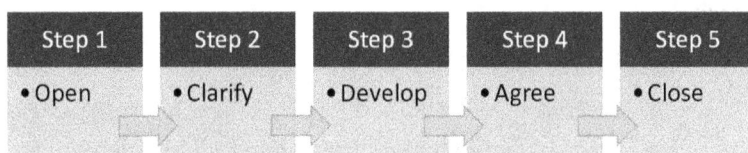

Step 1	Step 2	Step 3	Step 4	Step 5
• Open	• Clarify	• Develop	• Agree	• Close

Let's take a closer look of each of the five steps, see how they relate to project communications, and explore an example of each.

The first step is OPEN. In this step, we address what the objective of this conversation is, and why it is important. Just like a "project objective," you could consider this step as your "communication objective." This is an opportunity to "open the dialogue." For example:

Step 1: OPEN

- *Today, I would like to hear your thoughts on how the team will achieve the project objective for the new accounting system. This new system will reduce our invoicing time by 30 days, and accelerate receiving customer payments.*

The second step is CLARIFY. In this step, we are gathering information by seeking details and sharing data about the project problem. This is an opportunity to ask questions, to identify roadblocks, and reveal any concerns. This step is essential for establishing clarity and gaining mutual understanding. For example:

Step 2: CLARIFY

- *We both agree that this is a very difficult project, and must be delivered on time, within budget, and according to project specifications. So let's look at the facts that we have. I don't want to miss anything.*

The third step is DEVELOP. In this step, we are developing ideas, leveraging our creativity, utilizing the expertise of others, and discussing what resources and support are needed to make these ideas a reality. This is an opportunity for you (as the project manager) to also share your ideas and suggestions. For example:

Step 3: DEVELOP

- *In order to achieve the project objective, we really need a high-performing project team. I would like to hear your ideas on this. What do you think it will take to be a high-performing team, and what additional resources do you think are needed?*

The fourth step is AGREE. In this step, we are putting together our action plan with specific dates, details, and alternatives if needed. This is an opportunity to show commitment and how progress on the action plan will be tracked. For example:

Step 4: AGREE

- *So let's agree to meet every Monday morning at 9 a.m. to review the action plan together, and make any necessary adjustments. I will send a calendar request for our weekly meetings.*

The fifth and final step is CLOSE. In this step, we want to summarize the important items that have been discussed, and to provide our support and encouragement. This is an opportunity to build confidence and trust. For example:

Step 5: CLOSE

- *Let's recap what we have decided. Do you have any questions?*
- *I have complete trust and confidence in you. I know that you will do an excellent job on this. You are the right person to handle this difficult situation.*

Throughout the five-step process, make sure that you are also:

Checking for understanding. In project conversations, there is often a lot of information to share and discuss. Getting "off track" can easily occur which can create misunderstandings and confusion. During the discussion, use the opportunity to "check in." Ask: "What have you just heard?" When someone repeats what you have said, this helps to check for understanding. (Later in the chapter, we will discuss seeking and giving feedback.)

Making procedural suggestions. In project conversations, we need to keep the discussion moving forward and on target. Remember that during Step 1, we stated the purpose and importance when we "opened" the discussion. In order to achieve your conversation objective, you may need to adjust the dialogue along the way.

Using this approach can help guide your project communications and discussions to achieve clarity, gain understanding, align expectations, and deliver better results.

Figure 6.2 shows how these two elements—personal needs and practical needs—work together and are "essential" to the internal and external communications on the project.

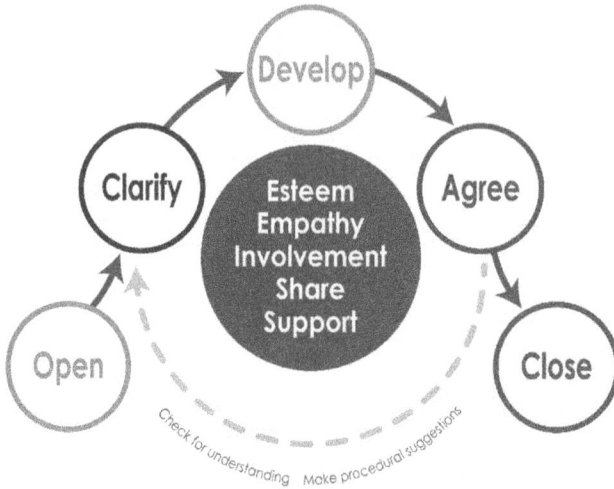

Figure 6.2 Interaction Essentials *developed by DDI. Reprinted with permission.*

©Development Dimensions International, Inc., 1986. All rights reserved. Reprinted with permission from Development Dimensions International, Inc.

Both of these questioning techniques can be used to provide a structure in managing communications within the project team (internal) or outside the project with stakeholders and other groups (external).[7]

Monitoring Project Communications

Monitoring communications in your project means evaluating the communications that are taking place, so that you can ensure you are achieving the intent of your project communications management plan. Even a project communications management plan that is executed fully, down to every e-mail and status report, may not be effective if the communications are not achieving their purpose. Two methods to do this are to measure the effectiveness of your project communications and to incorporate feedback loops.

Measuring the Effectiveness of Project Communications

Peter Drucker, well known for his innovative thinking in the way we do business, is often quoted as saying, "What gets measured gets managed."[8]

So how do we measure the effectiveness of our project communications management plan? Are there specific communication feedback techniques that project managers commonly use? How do we measure the success of effective communications within project teams and with other stakeholders? What actions do we take when things aren't working?

Great questions. Communication is known for being difficult to measure, as it is hard to prove a cause–effect relationship between communication and action. However, let's see if we can take a closer look at measuring the effectiveness of our project communications with helpful steps that we can take as project managers, team members, and project sponsors.

Before you start evaluating the effectiveness of your project communication, you need to determine *what, how,* and *when.*

WHAT: What are you measuring? What are the criteria for the measurement?

Start with the outcome you desire to achieve. The purpose of your project communications is to keep all stakeholders informed so that the project progresses smoothly and ultimately achieves its objectives. Different elements of your project communications management plan will do this in different ways. Stand-up meetings (see Chapter 7) are meant to keep the team informed. Status reports keep stakeholders outside the project team apprised of progress. When deciding what to measure, revisit the specific goals of each tactic in your project communications management plan. You are looking to measure whether your project communications are meeting your stated goals.

HOW: How will you measure it?

Depending on what you define as your outcomes, there are several approaches to measuring communications:

Usage data: Technology applications lend themselves most readily to quantitative measures. Intranet sites can track analytics on who is using the site, how often, and for how long. E-mail marketing applications can track open and clickthrough rates. Online collaboration tools can track which team members are most active and where the most conversations are happening. Correlating this data with project deliverables and deadlines can potentially show areas where communications are, or are not, accomplishing the desired objectives.

Surveys: If you want to know if communications are working for the people who receive them, just ask. Surveys can range from simple feedback questions that provide qualitative and/or anecdotal information to more formal surveys with quantitative results. You can survey directly about project communications, or about desired outcomes like increased support for the project among stakeholders.

Planned versus actual communications: Your project communications management plan should outline your different communication tactics and how often you plan to use them—for example, status reports will be sent every 2 weeks. Measure how closely you are keeping to the plan and compare that with other project outputs. As with usage data, you may be able to correlate your communication efforts with positive or negative aspects of the project's progress.

WHEN: When will you measure its effectiveness?

It is a good idea to start measuring early, and then measure frequently throughout the life of the project. If you don't discover until the end of the project that your communications were ineffective, you have missed an opportunity—and possibly hindered your project's success in the process. If your initial findings lead you to make changes to what or how you communicate, then measure again to ensure that the changes you made have actually improved your project communications. Project communications should be iterated and refined to ensure they are effectively informing all of your stakeholders.

Feedback Loops

Communication is not a one-way street. Sending an e-mail, for example, is only half of the process. Have you ever sent an e-mail and not received a response? You might ask yourself, "Did the person receive my message? Did they read it? Did they understand it?" You are uncertain whether your message has been delivered because you have not gotten *feedback* from the receiver. Feedback from the receiver, such as a response to your e-mail, "closes the loop" between the sender and receiver of the message.

Why is a feedback loop important? It verifies that what you intended to communicate is what is actually understood by the receiver. Consider the basic sender–receiver communication model (Figure 6.3).

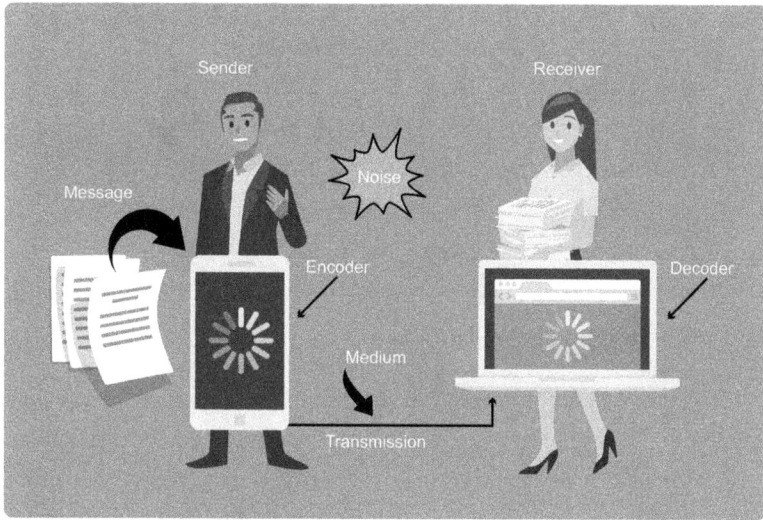

Figure 6.3 Basic sender–receiver communication model

- Sender: You are the sender, the person who initiates the message.
- Encoder: You type the message into the device (computer, phone, etc.) using text, numbers, symbols, etc. to create your message.
- Transmission: You send your message via some form of communication, such as e-mail.
- Noise: There are obstacles or barriers that could interfere with you sending your message, with the receiver not getting your message, or with the receiver not understanding your message. There can be many causes of noise, which vary from inadequate technology systems to lack of clarity in your message.
- Decoder: The receiver now has your message on his/her screen.
- Receiver: This is the person you intended to receive your message.

The feedback part of the process occurs in reverse, with the receiver responding to the sender to ensure that he/she actually understood what you intended to communicate. Figure 6.4 shows the sender–receiver communication model that includes the feedback loop.

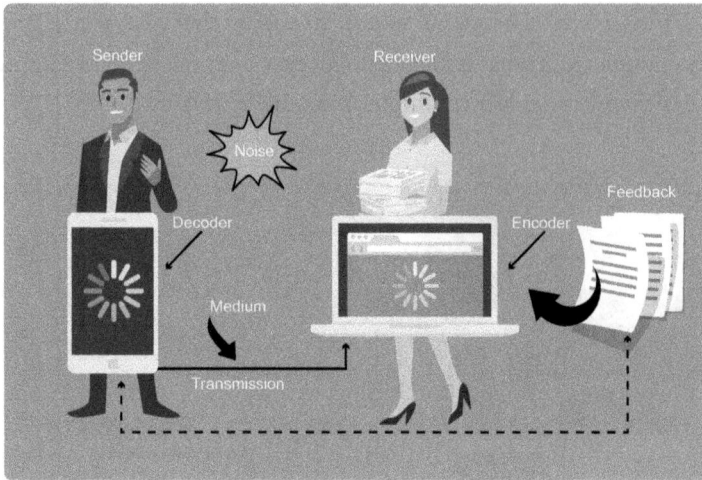

Figure 6.4 Closing the feedback loop

Whether you are the sender or receiver of the message, one essential element in feedback is closure. Too often, there are items left unacknowledged, unclear, or unresolved in a conversation or interaction. For example: A stakeholder has a positive experience with a project team member and sends a note of recognition to the project manager. There is no response. Did the project manager receive it? Did he or she not agree with it? Does he or she have a conflict with the stakeholder? The item is left unresolved until the project manager responds. Even worse, the stakeholder has a negative experience because there is no feedback, which may cause the stakeholder to move toward resisting the project (see Chapter 3). This is why Step 5 (Close) in the conversation guidelines outlined earlier in this chapter is so important. We need to be crystal clear that the subject has been closed, agreed upon, and next steps decided.

How do you ask for feedback? According to Tom Peters, coauthor of *In Search of Excellence*, the "four most important words in management are…'what do you think?'"[9] These four words are critical in project communications. Asking people what they think is a powerful tool. It provides space for team members or stakeholders to address any remaining uncertainties they may have, and/or confirm their understanding of your message. It helps build trust by demonstrating that you value their personal and practical needs and want to ensure they are addressed by your message. Track the number of times you ask the project team or stakeholders, "What do you think?" It can make a big difference.

Finally, when engaging in a conversation or electronic exchange, check in with yourself using your own internal feedback loop. How can you be sure you are communicating what matters? Ask yourself: Am I adding value to this discussion? Is it a fact or my opinion? Is it relevant to the topic? Has someone already said this, and I am just repeating what someone else said? Consider Figure 6.5 which shows the concept of W.A.I.T., or Why Am I Talking? This concept can also be applied to Why Am I Typing? It can be a valuable exercise to help you determine whether your communications are purposeful.

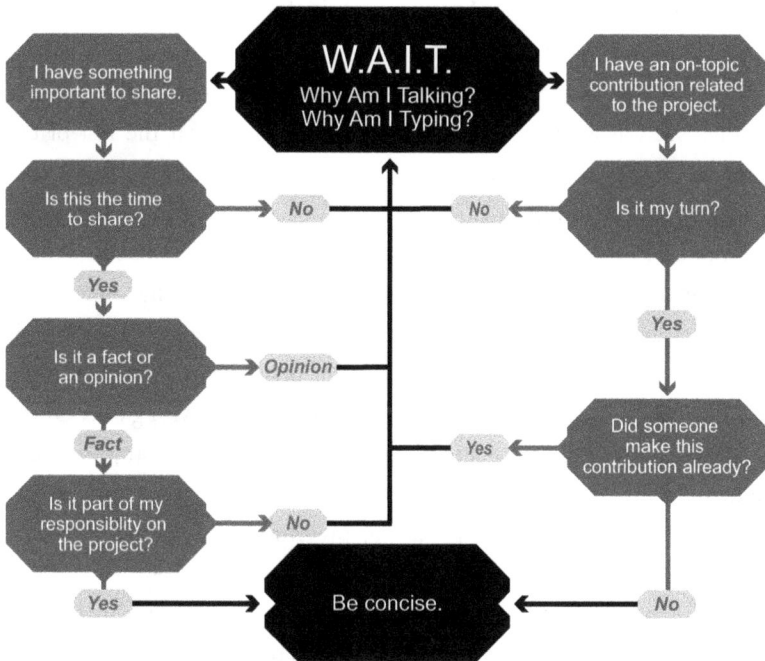

Figure 6.5 W.A.I.T. Why Am I Talking? Why Am I Typing?

Lessons Learned and Retrospectives

In managing projects, we constantly hear, "document your lessons learned." In agile project teams, lessons learned are called retrospectives. Regardless of the terminology, the key is to document and communicate what worked well and what needs improvement on the project. Simply writing these lessons down is not enough. They need to be used—by your team and by other project teams—to help avoid pitfalls and problems that have already been encountered, and to share effective processes and ideas so they can benefit future project teams.

When should you document (and communicate) lessons learned? Most often, teams do it (if at all) at the *end* of the project. Wrong. Lessons learned should be documented and communicated *throughout* the project. For example, in Week 3 of the project, the team experiences a situation that resulted in a "learning moment"—or a lesson learned. This is documented in their Week 3 status report and provides an opportunity to use this learning moment for the rest of the project. For agile projects, the team may conduct retrospectives at various intervals in the project. Regardless of timing, it is about reviewing, documenting, learning, and making improvements.

Lessons learned captured early in the project can ensure that positive results, such as a practice that works, are continued for the rest of the project. Or if there are lessons learned with a negative result, it could raise concerns to stop doing it, or make immediate adjustments, as the project continues. Either way, capturing and communicating lessons learned is a key element in managing and monitoring project communications.

Recall too that lessons learned can be about your project communications. Perhaps a team member missed a deadline because there were conflicting versions of a schedule and she looked at the wrong one. Or the sponsor came to you in a panic because he was asked for a project update and could not locate the most recent status report. Update your project communications management plan to prevent these issues from occurring again, but don't forget to also document them as lessons learned. That way you won't just improve your communications on this project, but on future projects as well—your own and others'.

Consider adding a "lessons learned" category to your status report. This way, key information and learning moments are documented throughout the project and can be easily referenced when the project closeout meeting occurs.

Putting It into Practice

Here are a few practical tips, fun activities, and useful ideas for how you can implement the concepts in this chapter into your project environment.

Note that ideas listed in one type of team may be adapted to other teams. Be creative. Use these as a starting point. Add your own ideas to build your communications toolkit.

Managing and monitoring project communications	
Traditional project teams	• Introduce the five-step approach to managing conversations to your project team. Conduct role-playing activities where each team member has the chance to be on the giving and receiving end of the conversation. • Set a feedback requirement with your team that all communications from other team members or stakeholders must be acknowledged within a set time limit (e.g., 24 hours). After 2 weeks, meet with the team and ask them to share the results and impact of using this technique. • Set up a reward system—gold stars on a publicly displayed board, points toward meaningful prizes, etc.—for team members who ask, "What do you think?"
Agile project teams	• Because of the rapid nature of agile teams, make sure you set aside time to close the feedback loop, and not leave items unresolved. • Look for simple ways to communicate status on your project. It saves time and reduces uncertainty. • Use retrospectives to measure the effectiveness of your communication activities and efforts.
Virtual project teams	• Virtual teams often use technology-based collaboration tools that provide analytics on usage. Find out the most active people and workstreams, and ask those team members why they are so active. Challenge less active team members or working groups to communicate more. • Develop a brief survey about communications on your current project, and send it to your stakeholders. In reviewing the results, take note of why some stakeholders may be more satisfied with project communications than others. • Post lessons learned in a searchable database with easy access for everyone. Organize content by categories with similar items grouped together for ease of reference.

Summary

Once you have developed your project communications management plan, you are now ready to start using it to manage and monitor your project communications. Addressing the personal needs *and* practical needs of the project team and stakeholders is an excellent place to start.

Have a structure for conducting your discussions so that you stay on track and achieve your communication objectives. Throughout your conversations or interactions, work toward ensuring understanding by all parties and make adjustments depending on the responses in the discussion or exchange.

To measure the effectiveness of your project communications, determine *what* you will measure and its criteria, *how* you will measure it, and *when* you will measure its effectiveness. Giving and getting feedback ensures what you intended to communicate is what is actually understood by the receiver. Asking questions like, "What do you think?" or, "What did you just hear?" are effective ways to get input and feedback. Use your own internal feedback process to make sure that you are adding value with each e-mail, meeting, or discussion. Documenting lessons learned and conducting regular retrospectives are essential in demonstrating if your project communications are working—or not.

Key Questions

1. In your project communications, how are you addressing the personal needs and practical needs of your project team members, sponsor, and stakeholders? Write them down.

2. Count the number of times you ask your project team members and/or stakeholders, "What do you think?" Track the results. Share with others.

3. What techniques are you using to measure the effectiveness of your project communications? List them. Note which techniques are working, and where changes are needed.

Notes

1. Whyte (1950), p. 174.
2. Project Management Institute (2017), *PMBOK® Guide*, 6th ed., p. 359.
3. Project Management Institute (2017), *PMBOK® Guide*, 6th ed., p. 647.
4. Project Management Institute (2017), *PMBOK® Guide*, 6th ed., p. 367.

5. Byham and Wellins (2015), p. 49.
6. Byham and Wellins (2015), p. 76.
7. ©Development Dimensions International, Inc., 1986. All rights reserved. Reprinted with permission from Development Dimensions International, Inc.
8. Prusak (2010), https://hbr.org/2010/10/what-cant-be-measured.
9. Peters (2010), p. 155.

References

Byham, T. M. and R. S. Wellins. 2015. Your First Leadership Job: How Catalyst Leaders Bring Out the Best in Others. Hoboken, NJ: Wiley.

Peters, T. J. 2010. *The Little Big Things: 163 Ways to Pursue Excellence.* New York, NY. Harper Collins.

Project Management Institute. 2017. *A Guide to the Project Management Body of Knowledge.* 6th ed. Newtown Square, PA: Project Management Institute.

Prusak, L. October, 2010. "What Can't Be Measured." *Harvard Business Review.* https://hbr.org/2010/10/what-cant-be-measured.

Wigert, B. and N. Dvorak. May, 2019. "Feedback Is Not Enough," *Workplace Newsletter,* https://www.gallup.com/workplace/257582/feedback-not-enough.aspx.

Whyte, W. H. September, 1950. "Is Anybody Listening?" *Fortune.*

CHAPTER 7

Using Project Communication Tools

The more elaborate our means of communication, the less we communicate.[1]
—Joseph Priestley, 18th century theologian, philosopher,
chemist, grammarian, teacher

It seems like every day, a new device, software program, mobile application, or widget is announced that will improve whatever we are doing. Everything is the "latest and greatest." With each new announcement, our communication seems to become more sophisticated, more complicated, more expensive—and perhaps more intimidating. The end result is that we may actually start communicating less—at least, communicating less in person.

This chapter looks at various communication tools and how to select the right tool relative to the size and complexity of your project, the experience and location of your project team, and the needs of the team, stakeholders, and organization.

The purpose of this chapter is to help you:

- Consider what goes into choosing the right communication tools for your project
- Examine the purpose and benefits of different project communication tools
- Understand the importance of being knowledgeable about whatever communication tools you use for your project
- Put it into practice: Using communication tools in traditional, agile, and virtual project teams

As a reminder, in Chapter 1 we defined project communication tools as any mechanism or strategy to exchange information, reduce uncertainty, engage stakeholders, build trust, generate support for the project, and, ultimately, deliver project and team success.

From a different perspective, Merriam Webster defines a tool as:

- a handheld device that aids in accomplishing a task
- something (such as an instrument or apparatus) used in performing an operation or necessary in the practice of a vocation or profession
- a means to an end
- natural ability[2]

Yes, your natural ability is also a communication tool!

Choosing the Right Communication Tool

Our emphasis in this section is on the process and importance of choosing the right tool, rather than focusing on specific, brand-name products or services. Think about Simon Sinek's approach of the Golden Circle (shown in Figure 7.1) as described in his book, *Start with Why*. The concept is to start with WHY, then look at HOW, then answer WHAT.[3]

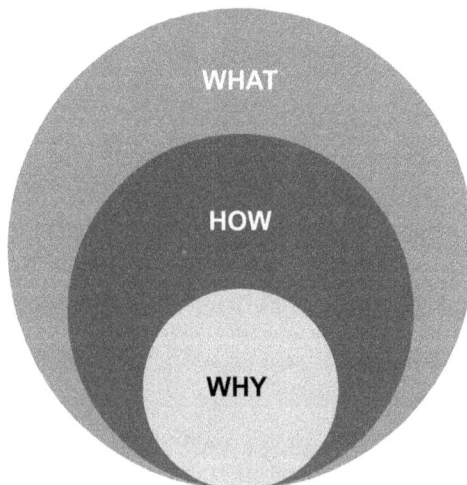

Figure 7.1 The Golden Circle

Sinek describes the approach in relation to organizational success, but we can use the same approach when selecting project communication tools:

- WHY—the reason or purpose. Why are we addressing this communication problem? Why is this an issue? Why is this important?
- HOW—differentiating factors. How do the different features, capabilities, or uses address our project communication needs? How will this tool solve a need or enhance our project communication abilities?
- WHAT—the product or mechanism. What project communication tool is the best solution? What result or change in our project communications do we expect to see?

The Why

Many times, we don't stop to consider the *why*. Usually, we start with the tool (the what) and even look at the features (the how), before we address the need (the why). For example: Let's say you see a demonstration of a new carpet cleaner (the what). You love the features, accessories and the high-quality cleaning it does (the how), and you buy it—except you don't have any carpets to clean (missing the why)! The same is true in projects. We get a new communications tool. We start using it. We then discover it does not meet our communication needs. This creates even greater communication problems on the project: more misunderstandings, more frustration, more waste of time and resources, and more uncertainty.

How can we avoid this? By starting with the *why*! Why are we addressing this communication need? Why is this an issue? Why is this important to the project, team, and stakeholders? Focus first on the *why*—the reason or the purpose. Once these questions are answered, the next steps of *how* and *what* will logically follow.

The How

Next, establish a list of criteria based on your project needs, organization, team, budget, and other influencing factors. In the *Buyers' Guide for Beginners Selecting PM Software*, author Elizabeth Harrin recommends focusing "on the criteria *that matter*" when selecting the right product or tool.[4] These criteria are the *how*—how the tool can accomplish the *why*.

Harrin provides a sample criteria list (as shown in Exhibit 7.1). This is an excellent place to begin. Take a look at the list and modify it to build your own set of selection criteria.

Exhibit 7.1

Sample criteria to consider when selecting a project tool[5]

- Task management: How is managing tasks handled? Is it a simple tool or do we need complex features?
- Tracking: How does the tool track time, tasks, budgets, resources, and progress?
- Visibility: How are dashboards and project reports shown?
- Accessibility: How is the online access?
- Mobility: How does a mobile app help our project team manage their work?
- Features: How are collaboration features handled, like discussions or online chats?
- Security: How is security addressed so that we know our data is safe?
- Integration: How easy is it to integrate with our current environment including compatibility with other products we use?
- Usability: How is the usability? Is it simple to use so that the team can start using it immediately?
- Cost: How does it fit within our budget?

Why is this important? A criteria list provides you with a focused roadmap for your selection process so that you don't get off track with criteria that *do not matter*.

In evaluating tools, you also need to consider how the communication takes place—is it synchronous (meaning real-time or contemporaneous) or asynchronous (not interactive or not at the same time)? A combination of both synchronous and asynchronous communication tools is required for all types of project teams and stakeholders. Table 7.1 provides examples and considerations for both types.

Table 7.1 Synchronous and asynchronous communications[6]

Type	Example	Note
Synchronous communication	Project team members or stakeholders are engaged in the dialogue together (either electronic or verbal). Examples include online chat sessions or face-to-face conversations.	Participants are in the same place at the same time (i.e. face-to-face) or different place at the same time (i.e. online chat or teleconference). There is two-way communication with an immediate response.
Asynchronous communication	Project team members or stakeholders are *not* engaged in a dialogue. Examples include sending an e-mail, distributing an internal memo, or posting information on the project website.	Participants are communicating at different times. (Note that this does not mean different time zones!) They may be in the same place, but not talking with each other. Or they may be in different places (remote locations). This is one-way communication waiting (hopefully) for a response or acknowledgement, or making others aware that the information is now available.

Figure 7.2 provides a graphic depiction of asynchronous and synchronous communications.

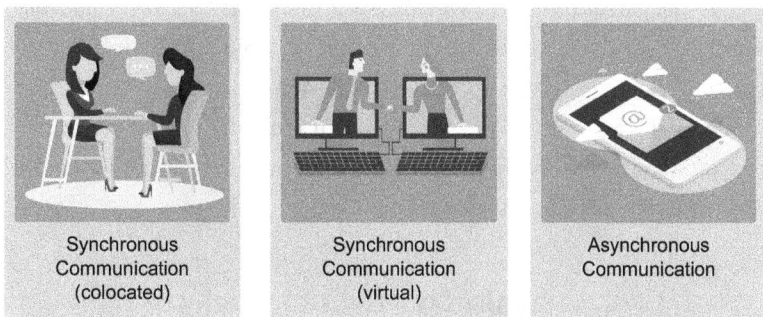

| Synchronous Communication (colocated) | Synchronous Communication (virtual) | Asynchronous Communication |

Figure 7.2 Depiction of synchronous and asynchronous communications

Once you have established your criteria list and have considered the need for synchronous and asynchronous communications, the next step is to prioritize the criteria in order of importance. Categorize the features into three groups:

- Group 1: Criteria you must have
- Group 2: Criteria you would like to have
- Group 3: Criteria you don't need

Using the template in Table 7.2, you can take your criteria list and populate your priorities. If you need a place to get started, consider using the criteria shown in Exhibit 7.1.

Table 7.2 Template for tool selection criteria and priority

Criteria	Must have	Would like to have	Do not need
1.			
2.			
3.			
4.			

Why is this important? Putting together a criteria list and establishing priorities *before* looking at the actual communication tools—regardless of the type of tool—will help you throughout the selection process and increase the probability of choosing and using the most effective tools that fit your project needs.

The What

Now that we have looked at the *why* and the *how*, it is time to look at the *what*—the actual project communication tools that you might consider. The goal here is to find and select tools that can accomplish the *why* while meeting all of the criteria you have established in the *how*. The next section provides an overview of several types of project communication tools for consideration. This is a partial list as there are many options available, and those options are changing all the time.

Communication Tools for Projects

Let's look at some of the *many* different types of communication tools project teams could use. Since technology, products, and services are constantly changing, we are taking a generic approach, looking at different categories of tools rather than referencing or endorsing any specific product.

In managing projects and working with project teams and stakeholders, you should be using a *collection* of project communication tools. Each tool in your collection has its own purpose and benefits. When it comes to project communications, there is no "one size fits all!"

To get started, we will look at five general categories of project communication tools. There may be other classifications, but let's start with these. Table 7.3 displays these five categories in the order in which we will address them in this section.

Table 7.3 Categories of project communication tools

1	2	3	4	5
Technology	Project documents	Presentations and templates	Meetings	Talents and strengths

Technology

Choosing the most effective technology must be done carefully. This is not a simple process. It is "influenced by the organization's budget, the nature of the team task, and members' access to various technologies."[7] There is urgency. There is confidentiality. There is availability and compatibility. There is knowledge and ability. The process is not easy.

Collaboration Software

PC Magazine defines collaboration software as "many different kinds of apps and services that handle everything from video conference calls to letting two people type on a document at the same time."[8] When a team needs to collaborate, use collaboration software tools that allow for interactive discussions (such as online chat rooms or instant messaging) or the ability to jointly work on the same document. It will increase productivity with people working together, talking, and communicating (synchronous). When information needs to be shared, collaboration websites provide a resource for storing, communicating, and sharing project information (asynchronous). The benefit is that the project team and authorized stakeholders can use the website—at their convenience—for accessing the most current information on the project. In addition, collaboration tools today are very robust and can be especially useful for teams who are not colocated. They also cut down significantly on e-mail clutter.

Video Conferencing

The value in using a video conferencing tool as a communication method is that you can *see* everyone. Consider it another form of face-to-face meeting. You benefit from the verbal communication, as well as seeing the nonverbal communication of gestures, body language, reactions, or level of participation. Furthermore, you can share a screen to show participants documents, presentations, videos, and other information which can facilitate even greater understanding and collaboration. The chat feature within many video conferencing tools provides an added mechanism for asking questions, getting clarification, and engaging online with other participants. The downside of video conferencing is that not everyone has the required bandwidth, or some may have difficulty accessing it or may not know how to use it effectively.

Teleconferencing

Conducting a phone meeting, or teleconference, among people who are not colocated is another communication tool. The benefit is that it is easier to schedule as it involves less complicated technology than a video conference call. Many teleconferencing and video conferencing tools also allow the meeting to be recorded so that team members who are absent can listen to it at a later time. Teleconferencing requires an excellent facilitator to manage the conversation so that participants are not talking all at the same time and the conversation (and agenda topics) keeps moving forward. A downside of these tools is that you can only *hear* the participants; you cannot *see* them.

E-mail

While e-mail is part of our daily routine, it is considered one-way communication (asynchronous). You send a message. Then you wait. And wait. And wait until you get a response, if any. E-mail should be used for *documenting* conversations, not *conducting* conversations. The benefit of e-mail is that it provides you with project documentation. The downside of e-mail is urgency (others may not respond as quickly as you need) and understanding (the tone of your written message may be different from the tone of how your message is read). In working on projects, look for tools that enable a two-way dialogue, not one-way. Remember: Just because you hit the "send" button on an e-mail does not mean that you have actually communicated.[9]

Just because you hit the "send" button on an e-mail does not mean that you have actually communicated.

Social Media

Using social media tools to communicate in a project is becoming more prevalent. Social media provides an avenue for sharing project information with stakeholders in a public, low-cost, and easily accessible way. This can be beneficial in large projects that affect members of the broader external community as a means to provide them with current information about the project status and how it affects them as it progresses. It also provides stakeholders with a means of providing feedback, and can be measured through engagement metrics available in many social platforms. However, social media is not the right tool for every project and every stakeholder group. Carefully consider the why, how, and what of using social media as a tool, and ensure it satisfies your tool selection criteria before moving forward.

Project Documents

Project Reports

How often do you hear a response to a question that sounds like, "Didn't you read the report?" or, "It's in the report!" If you are hearing this feedback, it likely is an indication that you are not meeting your stakeholders' communication needs by simply sending a report. Just because we put something in a report does not mean that we have effectively communicated the information.

Just because we put something in a report does not mean that we have effectively communicated the information.

In fact, the report is simply for documentation purposes. Just because we wrote it, it doesn't mean that people read it! If you know there is information in the report that certain stakeholders need to know, communicate it separately. At minimum, when you send the report, add an introductory note that uses bullet points to highlight specific aspects of the report you want to ensure they see. The benefit of project reports is that critical project information has been documented. The challenge: making sure that project reports, decision logs, issue logs, and other reports have a purpose and are being used (and read)!

Project Schedule

One of the most powerful tools we have for communicating about the project is the project schedule (see Figure 7.3 for an example of a project schedule). The project schedule is highly detailed and communicates the tasks, milestones, planned and actual start/end dates, durations, dependencies, resources, and other detailed information. It brings the pieces (information) from other sections of the project plan into one place—the schedule. To improve your project communications, consider printing the project schedule as a large wall chart, or post it on a virtual team wall. As you start doing the work on the project, mark your project schedule in different colors. When a task is late, communicate this by highlighting the task in a bright color with a large arrow or circle. When a task is completed early, communicate this by highlighting the task on the schedule in a different bright color and add an icon (star, exclamation point, etc.). The benefit of having a marked-up project schedule that is visible to everyone is communicating progress, problems, and commitment. Visibility is an excellent communication tool. For example, if you are assigned a task and it is late, it is circled for everyone to see! And for those tasks that are completed early or for other achievements, it is important to communicate and celebrate successes (large and small) throughout the life of the project.

Milestone Schedule

When you need to communicate a high-level view of the project schedule, a milestone schedule can be a great communication tool. By definition, a milestone schedule is "a type of schedule that presents milestones with planned dates."[10] Figure 7.4 is an example of a milestone schedule. Notice the difference in the level of detail in the milestone schedule (Figure 7.4) from the project schedule (Figure 7.3). The benefit of using a milestone

Task Name	Duration	Start	Finish	Preds	Resource Names
ABC COURSE DEV	**32 days**	**Wed 7/17/19**	**Thu 8/29/19**		
1 Course Design	**15 days**	**Wed 7/17/19**	**Tue 8/6/19**		
1.1 Determine 8 weekly topics	2 days	Wed 7/17/19	Thu 7/18/19		SME
1.2 Select textbook and assign weekly reading	2 days	Fri 7/19/19	Mon 7/22/19	3	SME
1.3 Select other learning materials	4 days	Tue 7/23/19	Fri 7/26/19	3,4	SME
1.4 Identify instructional media requirements	1 day	Mon 7/29/19	Mon 7/29/19	5,3	SME,ID
1.5 Define discussion question topics	5 days	Tue 7/30/19	Mon 8/5/19	6	SME,ID
1.6 Course Design Review	1 day	Tue 8/6/19	Tue 8/6/19	7	SME,ID,Dir
Course Design Complete	0 days	Tue 8/6/19	Tue 8/6/19	8	
2 Create Assignments	**8 days**	**Wed 8/7/19**	**Fri 8/16/19**		
2.1 Write assignments	3 days	Wed 8/7/19	Fri 8/9/19	8	SME,ID
2.2 Create rubrics	3 days	Mon 8/12/19	Wed 8/14/19	11	SME,ID
2.3 Develop answer keys/instructor notes	1 day	Thu 8/15/19	Thu 8/15/19	12	SME
2.4 Assignments Review	1 day	Fri 8/16/19	Fri 8/16/19	13	SME,ID,C
Assignments Complete	0 days	Fri 8/16/19	Fri 8/16/19	14	
3 Instructional Media	**12 days**	**Wed 8/7/19**	**Thu 8/22/19**		
3.1 Write scripts	5 days	Wed 8/7/19	Tue 8/13/19	8	Scriptwri
3.2 Design media / film	3 days	Wed 8/14/19	Fri 8/16/19	17	MediaDe
3.3 Produce media	3 days	Mon 8/19/19	Wed 8/21/19	18	MediaPrc
3.4 Instructional Media Review	1 day	Thu 8/22/19	Thu 8/22/19	19	SME,ID,N
Instructional Media Complete	0 days	Thu 8/22/19	Thu 8/22/19	20	
4 Build Course	**5 days**	**Fri 8/23/19**	**Thu 8/29/19**		
4.1 Load course into LMS	3 days	Fri 8/23/19	Tue 8/27/19	14,20	LMSAdmin
4.2 Structure gradebook	1 day	Wed 8/28/19	Wed 8/28/19	23	LMSAdm
4.3 Course Review	1 day	Thu 8/29/19	Thu 8/29/19	24	ID
Course Build Complete	0 days	Thu 8/29/19	Thu 8/29/19	25	
Course Development Complete	0 days	Thu 8/29/19	Thu 8/29/19	9,15,21	

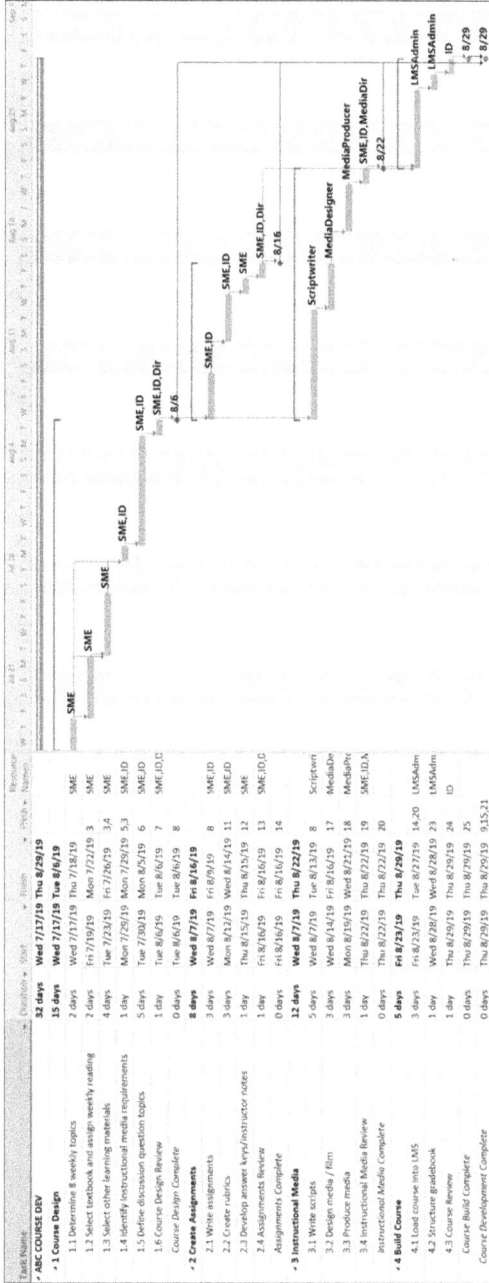

Figure 7.3 Project schedule example

Source: Debbie Austin, DBA, PMP

111

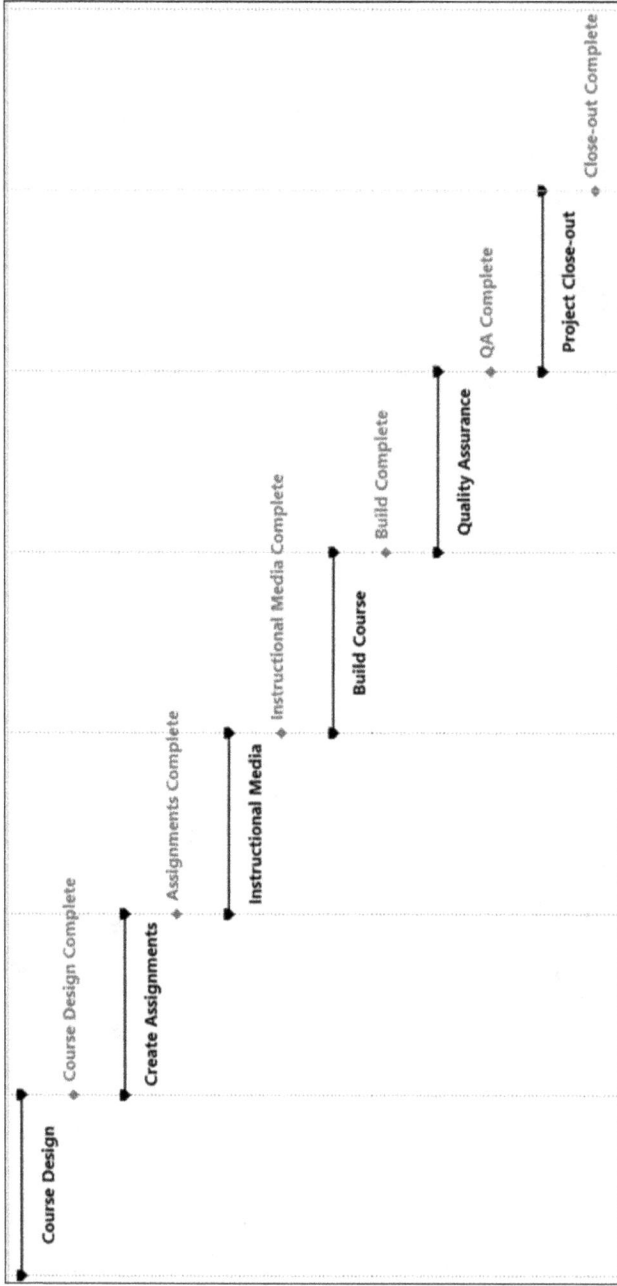

Figure 7.4 Milestone schedule example

Source: Debbie Austin, DBA, PMP

schedule as a communication tool is that sometimes key stakeholders, project sponsors, or management may only want a high-level view (or summary) of the status of key milestones, or points in time. Consider using a milestone schedule for communicating in these situations.

Status Reports

Status reports allow us to communicate project progress at regular intervals. Whether your document is called a status report, project update, or some other name, it is a vital communication tool. Without it, how would you know that progress is being made on the project? The frequency and formality of communicating project status will depend on your project. This should be documented in your team operating principles (see Chapter 4), and your project communications management plan would show additional details about status reports (see Chapter 5).

Status reports do not need to be complicated. They should be easy to read and preferably a maximum of one page (depending on the size and complexity of the project). Using a template (such as the one shown in Table 7.4) ensures that a constant format and consistent information is being communicated. Don't forget to add a section to your status report on recent lessons learned! Post your status reports on the collaboration website or in a shared folder for easy access by the project sponsor, project team, management, and other key stakeholders. Make sure that your stakeholders are receiving current information in the status reports, and not getting status reports with outdated details. The timing of your status report distribution should be outlined in your project communications management plan. The benefit in consistently using status reports is that they help answer the question, "Where are we on the project?" for everyone involved.

Kanban Board

The Kanban board is becoming a more common tool, particularly for agile project teams. Basically, it communicates what tasks need to be done (to do), what is being worked on (in progress), and what has been done (completed). There may be other elements you include on your Kanban board to fit your needs. Figure 7.5 shows an example of a simple Kanban

Table 7.4 Status report template

Project status report	**Status:** ☐ Green: On track (within cost, schedule, scope parameters) ☐ Yellow: In jeopardy ☐ Red: Off track
Submitted by:	
Role:	
Project name:	
Reporting period:	
Report date:	

Project objective

Project status	*Include color (green, yellow, red) and explanation*
Overall	
Scope	
Schedule	
Budget	
Other	

Tasks	*Completed since last report*

Tasks	*Working on (Progress on these tasks will be stated in next report)*

Issues/risks	*State problem, status, and next steps*

Comments	*Include any lessons learned*

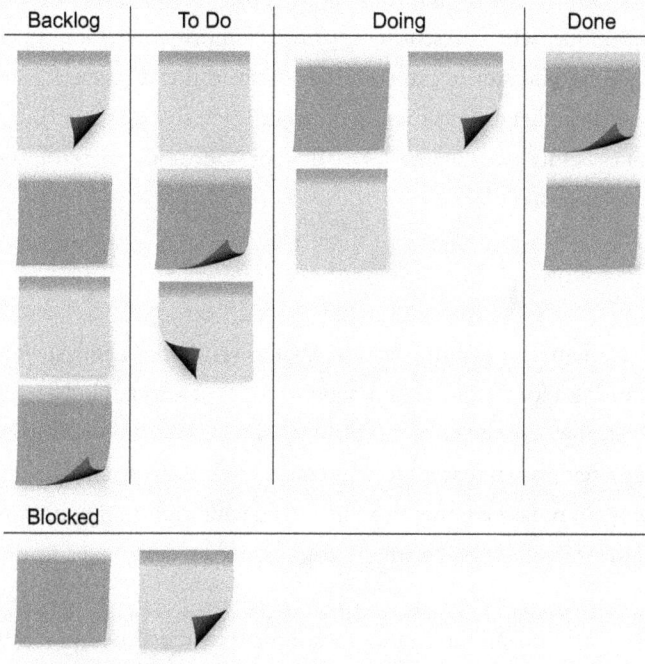

Figure 7.5 Example of a Kanban board

board. Each task is represented by a "card" and the card moves across the board as the work progresses. Consider it a visible status report or a different, more visual way to communicate workload on the project. The benefit is that it is a great visual to show *to do*, *doing*, and *done*. It also helps in showing how much work is waiting to be done, the need to establish priorities, and visibility on problems (or work that is stalled or blocked).

As with other tools, there is often software available to create a digital version. You can create a digital Kanban board or use a physical Kanban board. Use whatever method works best for your project team. The key is that the board is visible and current!

Presentations and Templates

Presentations

Tools such as face-to-face presentations, interactive webinars, podcasts, or videos provide an excellent opportunity for communicating project information. This is a time to use your presentation skills and facilitation techniques when presenting key project information. Graphs, charts, photographs, and stories can create very powerful and impactful images. The benefit is that you can engage the audience (see Chapter 3) and reduce uncertainty (see Chapter 2) by directly addressing any project questions or concerns.

Templates

There is a template or form for just about everything! Don't spend your time creating a form from a blank sheet of paper or screen. Find a template, modify it, then use the same template for similar interactions. The benefit in using a template is that it provides consistent messaging and branding to support your project communication. Spend your time on the communication content, and not on creating, designing, and redesigning a form.

> Spend your time on the communication content, and not on creating, designing, and redesigning a form.

Dashboards

Dashboards are an excellent communication tool to show a high-level overview of your project or multiple projects. They provide an opportunity to communicate key project information or a quick comparison of projects and the status of each. Figure 7.6 is an example of a project dashboard. Consider it an at-a-glance view of project status and high-level project information. The benefit in using a dashboard is that it is flexible depending on what information you choose to include and can be customized based on the needs of your stakeholders. Dashboards can also be used to keep everyone informed of how the project is progressing.

Meetings

Face-to-Face Meetings

Invest the time and money to have at least one face-to-face meeting for a project team, especially at the beginning of the project. Face-to-face

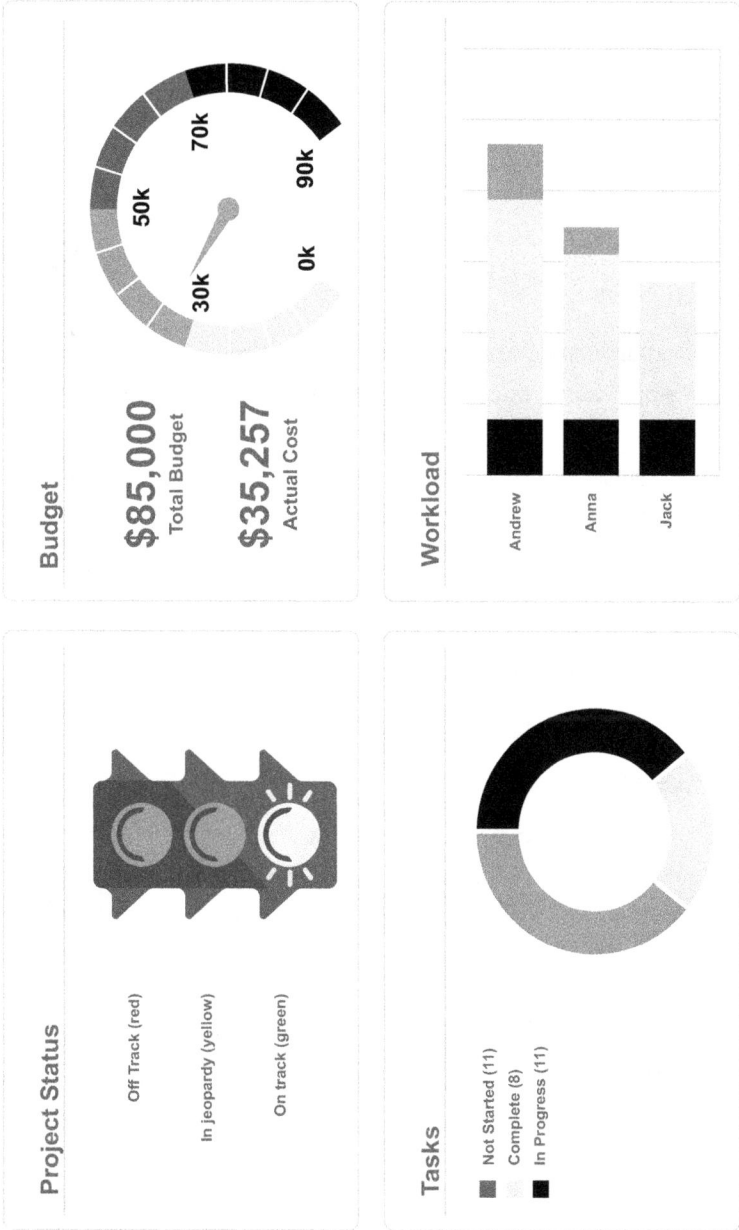

Budget

Project Status

Off Track (red)

In jeopardy (yellow)

On track (green)

70k

50k

30k

90k

0k

$85,000
Total Budget

$35,257
Actual Cost

Workload

Andrew

Anna

Jack

Tasks

Not Started (11)

Complete (8)

In Progress (11)

Figure 7.6 Example of a project dashboard

117

meetings are critical for all teams. Research shows that "when teams are unable to meet face-to-face—even once—they are less able to handle cultural differences and to understand and appreciate one another."[11] Don't underestimate the power and benefits of face-to-face meetings. They are crucial to project and team success! The downside of face-to-face meetings is the difficulty in getting everyone scheduled to attend at the same time, and the costs that may be associated with them. However, there are greater costs when face-to-face meetings are not held.

Stand-Up Meetings

Quick stand-up meetings are also an excellent communication tool, especially for agile project teams. Stand-up meetings are just that: participants stand. They do not sit down. The meeting is short and focused. In agile practice, stand-up meetings typically occur daily and last no longer than 15 minutes. In traditional or hybrid teams, these meetings may occur weekly and last longer. Regardless of the duration, the benefit of stand-up meetings is that they are consistent, short, and focused. It is an opportunity to quickly identify problems, prioritize items, and provide support where needed. Make sure that you have established ground rules for your stand-up meetings (see Appendix E).

Meeting Outcomes

When working with teams and conducting meetings, it is essential to communicate the meeting outcomes, goals, or intentions. Meeting outcomes should address the intended goal for the meeting, and expectations of what will be accomplished by the end of the meeting. Include the meeting outcomes on the meeting agenda and distribute the agenda well in advance of the meeting time. The benefit in clearly stating meeting outcomes is that everyone knows that their time and input is valued and respected, and can come prepared for focused discussions.

Stories

Stories use a narrative format to relate a specific project experience or example. One of the oldest forms of human communication, stories simulate experience rather than just conveying information. The benefit in using stories is that stories tap into stakeholders' emotions as well as their minds, which provides deeper engagement. Stories show us what *has happened* to others in similar projects, which helps reduce the uncertainty of what *could happen* in the current project. In the right situation, such as an initial project team meeting or a conversation with an unsupportive stakeholder, stories can be one of the most effective tools in your communication arsenal.

Talents and Strengths

Natural ability is mentioned in the Merriam Webster definition of tools. What is our natural ability? The Gallup organization and their Strengths philosophy defines natural abilities as "the ways in which a person naturally thinks, feels, and behaves."[12] Natural abilities include our talents and our strengths.

What is a talent? It is a natural ability that a person is born with.

What is a strength? It is taking a talent and enhancing it by investing the time and effort to grow one's skills and knowledge through learning and practice. This occurs over a person's lifetime. A strength is the developed ability "to consistently provide near-perfect performance"[13] in a given activity, including the activity of project communication.

A strength is the developed ability "to consistently provide near-perfect performance" in a given activity, including the activity of project communication.

Martha Buelt, author and a Gallup-Certified Strengths Coach, explains that when project team members understand their own talents (natural abilities), they can better communicate what they need in order to maximize the use of their own talents and strengths on the team. Furthermore, when each team member can understand and articulate their own talents, team members are better equipped to develop their strengths. (Remember that developing a strength means taking a talent—something you do well naturally—and investing time, skills, knowledge, and practice to turn that talent into a strength.)

How each project team member develops their own specific communication strengths will vary depending upon the person's talents and the opportunities available to them for developing their talents into strengths. The following are general examples of project team members who are engaging in the process of developing and using their communication strengths on their project teams:

- If a project team member has the natural talent of "naturally understanding how people feel,"
  - then he can acquire and invest the knowledge of "what goes into asking good questions" into his talent
  - to develop a strength for "creating an environment in which team members can communicate how they feel" about the progress of the project.

- If a project team member has a natural talent to "write lists to keep track of project details,"
  - then he can invest the skill of using a software program into his talent
  - to develop a strength for "communicating the progress of the project team by making those lists available to and usable by other project team members."

- If a project team member has a natural talent for seeing "multiple possible paths forward" and another talent for "choosing the best path forward,"
  - then she can invest in her talents by practicing the articulation of what she is thinking
  - to develop a strength for "communicating what she sees to the project team."

- If a project team member has a natural talent for "wanting to break down and test research and data,"
  - which she has already developed into a strength for "analyzing data which is relevant for her project team,"
  - then she can invest further in her talents and strengths by practicing effective written and/or verbal articulation of her analysis
  - to develop an additional strength for "communicating her analysis to the project team," so that the project team can effectively use her analysis in the team's decision-making processes.[14]

Project managers have a responsibility to create an environment in which team members can become more aware of the collective communication strengths of the team. Furthermore, project managers can facilitate the assignment of tasks based on each team member's talents and strengths, maximizing the team's communication strengths toward project and team success. The benefit in using our natural abilities (talents) and developing our talents into strengths as an effective project communication tool is leveraging what we do best!

Be Knowledgeable. Be Curious. Be a Learner.

With all of the technology and tools available to us, and the associated marketing and buzz that comes with them, it can be easy to think that the right tool will solve *all* of our project communications problems. Wrong. Even when you have the right tool, you still must use it—and use it effectively. A hammer won't pound in a nail by itself. You must do the work.

Regardless of the type and level of skills you and your project team members have in using communication tools (technical, facilitation, presentation, storytelling, writing abilities, etc.), it is important to keep your skills sharp. As new project communications tools are released and existing tools evolve, it is important to keep learning. As project teams and stakeholders become more diverse and global, it is important to learn new cultures. Learn new words. Practice new ways of communicating. Being on a project team is about the learning experience. Take advantage of this learning opportunity.

Growing your knowledge to effectively use the communication tools on your project is 100 percent in your control. However, keep in mind that tools are constantly changing, and so are your project communication needs. If a tool is no longer effective or not working for you and the team, discuss it together and make the necessary adjustments. Just because we have a tool does not make us good communicators.

Putting It into Practice

Here are a few practical tips, fun activities, or useful ideas for how you can implement the concepts in this chapter into your project environment. Note that ideas listed in one type of team may be adapted to other teams. Be creative. Use these as a starting point. Add your own ideas to build your communications toolkit.

Using project communication tools	
Traditional project teams	• At the start of team meetings, have each participant share a new feature or approach they have found useful with one of the team's project communication tools. • Designate an area, wall, or room where project information can be posted. Visuals can help the team stay focused on important details of the project. • Traditional teams often benefit from colocation. Where this occurs, encourage impromptu problem-solving as a group. It can be extremely effective in not only solving the problem, but also in communicating issues and creating awareness of potential issues.
Agile project teams	• While the tools are important, remember that *you* are the best communication tool on agile project teams. It is the team and their interactions that make agile teams successful. • Using stand-up meetings helps agile teams focus on what will be accomplished each day. This can significantly increase team collaboration and problem-solving. This level of communication also quickly builds trust. • Continually look for and use simplified tools in working with agile teams and stakeholders. Spend more time on the message and connecting, and less time on using the tool.
Virtual project teams	• Using technology to communicate is crucial on virtual teams. Make sure that everyone has easy access and the necessary knowledge to effectively use the technology tools. Invest in training, coaching, or technology super-users so that technical expertise is easily available. • Interview team members about their technology experiences. Ask them what communication tools they like and why, and what tools they don't like and why. Post the results. This will jumpstart your efforts in selecting tools that everyone will use. • Ensure that the virtual team doesn't rely solely on asynchronous communication tools. Plan regular phone or video meetings with the team, and encourage them to use the phone or video chat to connect with one another frequently. • Using chat tools allows team members to pop in (much like popping over to someone's cubicle) for a quick question. This is an effective way to simulate face-to-face interaction and can facilitate quick problem-solving and team cohesion.

Summary

When exploring different communication tools, it is best to start with *why* we need the tool, then *how* the tool can meet those needs, then *what* specific tool we should use. With the vast array of communication tools available, many of which are constantly changing and being updated, it is critical to establish (and prioritize) criteria when selecting project communication tools to best fit the project, team, stakeholder, and organization needs.

Selecting the right tool is as important as knowing how to use the tool. Make sure that your project communications toolkit is actually being used. If you need education, training, or coaching, get it. If a project communication tool is not working well, discuss it with the team and make the necessary adjustments. Your communication tools should be an asset to help your project communications, not a burden.

As we noted at the end of Chapter 2, trust is a critical factor in project success. Trust is not built just by using a tool. You must choose tools that meet the communication needs of stakeholders, and then use them to deliver the right messages to the right stakeholders at the right time—thereby building trust. Tools alone do not create good project communications.

Key Questions

1. What criteria would you put on your list when selecting a project communication tool for your project? How would you prioritize your criteria?

2. What is your project "story"? Share it with your team and colleagues or record it as a video. Get feedback from others.

3. Do you use your talents and strengths as a project communication tool? If yes, how do you use them in communicating effectively within the project team, and with other stakeholders? If no, how can you start using your talents and strengths more effectively?

Notes

1. Gupta (2008), p. 3.
2. Merriam-Webster Online, https://www.merriam-webster.com/dictionary/tool.
3. Sinek (2009), p. 37.
4. Harrin (2015).
5. Harrin (2015).
6. Smith (2012), https://www.imedicalapps.com/2012/05/synchronous-asynchronous-communication/.
7. DuFrene and Lehman (2016), p. 49.

8. Duffy (2019).

9. Tumlin (2013), p. 32.

10. Project Management Institute (2017), *PMBOK® Guide*, 6th ed., p. 711.

11. DuFrene and Lehman (2016), p. 17.

12. Rath (2007), p. 20.

13. Rath (2007), pp. 18–20.

14. Buelt Consulting, LLC, http://www.talentstrength.net.

References

Buelt Consulting, LLC. 2019. "Strengths-Based Talent Development." https://www.talentstrength.net/, (accessed July 22, 2019).

Duffy, J. August 22, 2019. "The Best Project Management Software of 2019." *PC Magazine*, https://www.pcmag.com/roundup/260751/the-best-project-management-software.

DuFrene, D. D. and C. M. Lehman. 2016. *Managing Virtual Teams*, 2nd ed. New York, NY. Business Expert Press.

Gupta, S. 2008. *Communication Skills and Functional Grammar.* New Delhi, India: University Science Press.

Harrin, E. December, 2015. "Buyers' Guide for Beginners Selecting PM Software." ProjectManager (blog), https://www.projectmanager.com/blog/buyers-guide-selecting-pm-software.

Merriam-Webster OnLine, s.v. "tool," https://www.merriam-webster.com/dictionary/tool, (accessed July 10, 2019).

Peters, T. J. 2010. *The Little Big Things: 163 Ways to Pursue Excellence.* New York, NY: Harper Collins Publishers.

Project Management Institute. 2017. *A Guide to the Project Management Body of Knowledge.* 6th ed. Newtown Square, PA: Project Management Institute.

Rath, T. 2007. *StrengthsFinder 2.0.* New York, NY: Gallup Press.

Sinek, S. 2009. *Start with Why: How Great Leaders Inspire Everyone to Take Action.* London, England. Penguin Books Ltd .

Smith, R. L. May, 2012. "Synchronous vs Asynchronous Communication and Why it Matters to You as a Doctor." iMedicalApps (blog), May 23, 2012, https://www.imedicalapps.com/2012/05/synchronous-asynchronous-communication/.

Tumlin, G. 2013. *Stop Talking, Start Communicating.* New York, NY: McGraw-Hill Education.

CHAPTER 8

Communicating Change

You can't build an adaptable organization without adaptable people—
and individuals change only when they have to, or when they want to.[1]
—Gary Hamel, American management consultant,
professor, and author

What is a project if not an engine for change? Whether the goal is to build a bridge, develop a new piece of software, transform an organization, or offer a new service or product to customers, the intent is that at the end of the project, something will be different than when it began. The opening pages of the *PMBOK® Guide* plainly state, "Projects drive change in organizations."[2]

At the same time, humans are naturally resistant to change. Employees can view change within an organization as a threat in many different ways—to their sense of control, to their feeling of competence in doing their job, to their expected workload and ability to complete everything asked of them, and even to their job security if the change could make what they do obsolete. They are uncertain, and depending upon whether and how their uncertainty is addressed, they could resist the change.

Change initiatives have a high rate of failure. Research shows that anywhere from 46 to 70 percent of organizational change efforts fail. Research also shows, however, that actively managing change positively impacts success in projects and organizational initiatives.[3,4] Organizations that excel at change management are five times more likely to integrate communication into their change management strategy, and are eight times more likely to implement and maintain changes.[5] If all projects involve change, then all projects should at least take into consideration the concept of managing and communicating change.

The purpose of this chapter is to help you:

- Understand change management, including three common models of managing change
- Describe how change management and project management work together
- Integrate change management into a project through communications
- Put it into practice: Communicating change in traditional, agile, and virtual project teams

What Is Change Management?

The Association for Change Management Professionals (ACMP) defines change as "the transition from a current state to a future state."[6] Current state and future state bookend the change—they are defined respectively as the conditions at the start when the change begins, and at the end once the benefits of the change have been realized.

Change management is "the practice of applying a structured approach to the transition of an organization from a current state to a future state to achieve expected benefits."[7] It focuses on the *people* within the organization who are affected by the change (all stakeholders, including the project team), and how to support them in accepting the change and transitioning to the future state.

How Do Change Management and Project Management Work Together?

The ACMP's Standard for Change Management specifically calls out the relationship between change management and project management.

> Project management methodologies typically emphasize the organization and management of resources and activities required to complete projects (deliver the change) within the defined scope, budget, timeline, and quality standards. Change management methodologies typically emphasize the people side of change and the activities required to prepare the organization for the delivered change, facilitate the transition from the old way of working to the future state, and embed the change as the new norm.[8]

As you can see, change management and project management differ, but overlap and are often interdependent. Integrating the two can help ensure that the objectives of the project (and the organization) are achieved. The responsibility for that integration varies depending on the context of the project.

1. Some organizations have change management offices, departments, and/or practitioners who specialize in this methodology. These practitioners are often part of the project team, and their role is to ensure the integration of change management principles into the life cycle of the project.
2. Other organizations expect communication professionals to address change management as part of their responsibilities within a project.
3. In many projects, change management or communication resources are not available to the project team. In these cases, it is the responsibility of the project team to ensure that change management principles are addressed.

This chapter is most applicable to the third situation and focuses on offering knowledge and communication strategies to project managers and team members who wish to incorporate change management methodology into their projects.

Change Management Models

There are a number of change management models available. Here is a brief overview of three of the most common: Kotter's eight-step model, Lewin's model, and the Prosci ADKAR model. While these models have different components and approaches, you'll see that they address similar concepts. Models like these can be useful frameworks to help you integrate change management principles into your project.

Kotter's Eight Steps

In his best-selling book *Leading Change*, John Kotter proposes an eight-step plan to help organizations change successfully. He based his approach on his personal experience and research with dozens of organizational change initiatives.

1. Create a sense of urgency around identified crises or opportunities.
2. Build a team to lead the change.

3. Develop a vision for the change, and a strategy to achieve the vision.
4. Get everyone on board by communicating the change vision.
5. Empower employees to action and remove barriers to change.
6. Generate short-term wins to build momentum and positive reaction to the change.
7. Continue the change momentum until the change vision is achieved.
8. Anchor the change within the organization's culture.[9]

Lewin's Model

Kurt Lewin's model for change is one of the earliest (1951), and while it is simple, it is still widely used today. He presented "Changing as Three Steps," or CATS:

Step 1: Unfreeze—People and organizations must prepare for change. One strategy to accomplish this is to demonstrate the discrepancy between the current state and the desired state.

Step 2: Change—People must change behaviors and embrace new roles and responsibilities. This is where change is put into action through new structures and processes.

Step 3: Refreeze—The new systems and behaviors are cemented into place. Support mechanisms like reward systems and reinforced cultural values can help accomplish this.[10]

The Prosci ADKAR Model

Jeff Hiatt, founder of the change management consultancy and training organization Prosci, developed a model that can be a useful tool in understanding and facilitating the five outcomes that individuals need to achieve in order to make change "stick."

- **A**wareness of the reasons/need for change
- **D**esire to participate in the change
- **K**nowledge about how to change
- **A**bility to implement the change
- **R**einforcement of the change[11]

Communicating Change

Incorporating principles of change management into your project communications is a natural fit. Managing change is much like managing uncertainty, which we have addressed throughout this book. The rest of this chapter outlines four change management concepts to build into your project communications. These concepts are drawn from the change management models described above, as well as the ACMP's Standard for Change Management.

1. The need for change
2. The effect of the change on stakeholders
3. Stakeholder support through the change
4. Change reinforcement

As you build your project communications management plan (see Chapter 5), use these four concepts to inform the content of your messages, timing, and other aspects of the plan. If you're struggling to understand just how these four concepts should play out in your project, ask your stakeholders to tell you. Involving them and asking for their input on the project can increase their commitment to and readiness for the change. Avenues for this include using sensing mechanisms like surveys or focus groups, or bringing in stakeholders as members of the project team, subject matter experts, testers, or other roles as appropriate.

To demonstrate this approach in practice, let's look at an example of a financial software implementation project. What concepts should the project team incorporate into project communications in order to ensure that the people affected by the change are ready, willing, and able to change?

The Need for Change

Employees want to know that the change is coming and why it's happening. This includes explaining why the change is necessary, how it is tied to the organization's overall strategy, and what the risks are of not changing. Research shows that successful companies align their projects with their overall purpose and strategy. This means explaining why the organization is undertaking the project, and how the project will help achieve organizational goals.

Communications about the need for change should start early in the project life cycle, and should clearly express the rationale for the project and relate it to the organization's goals and/or purpose. Much of this information can often be found in project documents like the project charter and business case, as well as organizational information like mission, vision, and/or values statements.

In our financial software implementation project example, communications should:

- **Address the need** for the new software: e.g., the old software no longer meets regulatory requirements around financial reporting; it could not be integrated into other business processes; or the software was being discontinued by the vendor.
- **Address the benefits** of the new software and how it aligns with organizational goals: e.g., the new software can provide a more seamless customer experience; it will eliminate manual processes that could introduce errors; or it will facilitate better financial reporting that helps the organization identify opportunities for growth.
- **Showcase sponsorship** for the change: Messages from leadership legitimize the change, reinforce its alignment with organizational goals, and reassure employees they will be supported through the change. A message from the chief financial officer could underscore the importance of the change and express a strong commitment to providing support to all employees affected by it. Supportive messages from immediate supervisors of directly impacted employees can also model a demonstrated need for and commitment to the change.

Stakeholder Impact

In line with the concept of "What's in it for me?" or WIIFM (see Chapter 3), communicating change means letting stakeholders know what to expect and when to expect it. Reduce their uncertainty and increase their trust in the project by answering their big questions.

Communications about what to expect should also begin early in the project life cycle and continue throughout. Don't expect to know and be able to share every aspect of this information up front; tell stakeholders what you can, when you can. Don't wait until every detail is finalized before you begin communicating, or stakeholders will begin to speculate on their own.

In our financial software implementation project example, communications should:

- **Explain what employees can expect** to see/experience during the implementation, i.e., give them a timeline for the software implementation, tell them how they will be supported, and reinforce why they should adopt the change (e.g., invoices will no longer be paid through the old system after the implementation date; employees will be valuable and key contributors to the organization's ongoing success by adopting the new system). Communicate that each person is important!
- **Address any anticipated risks and uncertainties**. If the new software will eliminate redundancies or create efficiencies, be clear about any impact on employee jobs. New software generally requires a learning curve, so reassure employees that proper training will be provided on how to use it.
- **Clearly outline expectations**. While training will teach employees how to use the new software, you also need to communicate when you expect them to use it, and the consequences of not using it. For example, all payment requests must be submitted through the new system effective March 1. Any requests submitted via the old system after March 1 will not be processed and will be sent back to the requesting employee.

Support for Making the Change

Employees need to know *how* to make the change you are asking of them. This includes communicating, educating, and training around roles and responsibilities, processes and tools, and desired behaviors. Initial communications should emphasize that support will be provided. Once the project is underway, you can provide additional details to stakeholders as they become available, including what form the support will take, and when stakeholders can expect it.

In our financial software implementation project example, you could use communications to:

- **Provide multiple educational tactics** to suit employees' different learning styles and give them a sense of control over how they will develop their knowledge. Formal training sessions can walk employees through the new software so that they can see how it works and practice using it. Follow-up videos and/ or written documentation can reinforce the individual steps required to process payments with the new software. An intranet forum can provide a place for users to ask questions and project team members to share tips and best practices. Challenge yourself to use the rule of seven (see Chapter 4) by communicating a number of options for employees to learn, and then reinforce their learning.

- **Acknowledge the difficulty of the change** by providing adequate and contextualized information. Is this software implementation merely a shift to a new platform, where much of the purpose and functionality is similar to the old system? Is it replacing an antiquated or manual process? Does it ask employees to know or understand more of the financial processes of the organization, such as how payments are applied against budgets? Be clear and be honest—you will diminish trust if you tell employees it will be a simple transition and then it turns out to be highly challenging for them.

- **Solicit and address feedback** about the change. Follow up with employees to identify any pain points they may be experiencing with the new software. Was a payment process not covered in your training? Did a software update change a specific step? Iterate and rerelease training and documentation to address those areas.

Change Fatigue

Change requires adaptation to something new for everyone affected by the project. The process of adaptation can be stressful, and when stakeholders are hit with wave after wave of change, that stress can lead to change fatigue. It is most common in organizational change initiatives where many aspects of the organization's operations and culture are expected to transition to a new state. According to a survey on organizational change initiatives by PricewaterhouseCoopers and the Katzenbach Center, 65 percent of respondents cited change fatigue as the biggest obstacle to change.[12]

Change fatigue happens when employees face too many changes at once or in rapid succession. They're often asked to do more, but rarely given clear prioritization of the different change initiatives. They may have seen similar change efforts fail in the past. Change fatigue is a form of burnout, and has many of the same consequences: increased absenteeism and presenteeism, lower engagement, and even increased turnover.

Change management approaches can help slow the development of change fatigue, and even combat some of its symptoms. However, even well-managed and effectively communicated change can wear people out if it goes on too long. If you think change fatigue could become an obstacle in your project, be sure to address the sources of change fatigue in your communications. However, you should consider it in your risk management planning as well, because *change fatigue is a risk to your project's success.*

Change Reinforcement

Reinforcement means ensuring the change is sustained. Human beings tend to revert back to old habits and patterns, so it's important to keep the change and its purpose in front of stakeholders even after the project itself is complete. This is one notable area where project management and change management diverge. Projects generally come to an end when the objectives of the project are achieved. Change management, however, continues after the end of the project to ensure that the outcomes are successfully adopted and integrated into the organization. It is an ongoing process to continue to influence stakeholders' engagement with and ability to implement the change.

In cases where change management processes are the responsibility of the project team, you may have limited ability to reinforce the change. Once the project is completed, team members move on to another project and/or return to their functional roles. However, you can include ongoing communications in your project close-out process. Recommend to the sponsor or other stakeholders who will manage the outcomes of the project that they continue communicating to keep stakeholders engaged and inhibit regression back to the former state. You can even provide recommendations of what those communications should look like and include a transition management plan in your project.

Once our example software implementation project is complete, continuing communications to reinforce the change can:

- **Celebrate change adoption**. Share success stories of individuals or groups who are successfully utilizing the new software. Hold an event to celebrate the rollout. Be sure to reinforce the goal of the change by connecting back to the goals of the project that were outlined in your initial communications about the need for the change, such as improved customer experience, cost savings, or reduced strain on organizational resources.
- **Build accountability into the process**. If you have clearly laid out expectations for implementation of the change, you should also establish and communicate accountability measures if those expectations are not met. Let stakeholders know that these expectations are being integrated into existing performance management processes.

Integrating Change Management into Your Communications Plan

Depending on the degree of change, the number of stakeholders, and the size and complexity of your project, it may be helpful to map your stakeholders to each of these four concepts and use the results to help you build your project communications management plan. The template shown in Table 8.1 can serve as a guide:

Table 8.1 Stakeholder change map template

Stake-holder	What should they know about the need for this change?	How will the project impact them?	What support will they need to take the actions required for project success?	What will reinforce the change with this group, even after the project ends?

Revisit and update this chart at least as often as you review and update your project communications management plan. As with many other aspects of the project, the answers to these questions can evolve over time as the project progresses.

The end goal of both project management and change management is for the project to succeed. But the integration of change management strategies into project management broadens the definition of success beyond simply completing the project on time, within budget, and within scope. Success means realizing the benefits of the project for the organization. "When applying change management, the project manager's goal is to deliver change that has been adopted (integrated into the organization's work), and to ensure that the intended benefits are on track to be delivered operationally over time."[13]

Putting It into Practice

Here are a few practical tips, fun activities, and useful ideas for how you can implement the concepts in this chapter into your project environment. Note that ideas listed in one type of team may be adapted to other teams. Be creative. Use these as a starting point. Add your own ideas to build your communications toolkit.

Communicating change	
Traditional project teams	• Challenge the project team to help implement the "rule of seven" (see Chapter 4). Have the team suggest seven different ways to communicate the change the project will bring. • At the initiation of the project, ask each team member to talk to one stakeholder about the project, and identify any uncertainties the stakeholder may have. Discuss the results and incorporate them into the project communications management plan. • Ask the project sponsor to create a brief video explaining how the change aligns with organizational objectives. Share the video with stakeholders, and post it on the project website.
Agile project teams	• Ask one team member to serve as the "change voice" on the team to verify that change is being communicated using the approaches in this chapter, and to speak up if it is not. Consider rotating the role with each sprint. • Choose at least one significant win for each sprint—reaching a major project milestone, receiving positive feedback from external stakeholders, reaching goals ahead of schedule—and share with all project stakeholders. Try telling it as a story (see Chapter 7). • Don't forget to focus on change management *within* the agile team. Agile projects by their nature involve significant change with each iteration. Ensure project team members understand what is changing with each sprint, why it is changing, and how they will be supported in accomplishing the goals of the next sprint.
Virtual project teams	• Ask team members to act as champions of the change. Provide talking points, posters, and other tactics that can help them talk about the change face-to-face with stakeholders in their various locations. • There is a learning curve when dealing with change. If a team member or stakeholder is struggling with understanding the change, look for different ways to share the message. Find out the preferred communication method of the team member or stakeholder, and adjust accordingly. • When working virtually, change fatigue can easily occur. As the project manager, make sure you are having regular conversations with each team member. As team members, make sure you are reaching out for help—from your project manager and your team colleagues.

Summary

Projects create change. Projects are the connectors between where we are now (current state) and where we want to be (future state). While there are different models of change management, three of the most common are Kotter's eight-step model, Lewin's model, and the Prosci ADKAR model. These models can help provide frameworks for integrating change management concepts into project communications—a task that often falls to the project team.

Change creates uncertainty. When there is too much change, or the change is continuous, change fatigue can occur. To minimize the uncertainty and fatigue, communication to help stakeholders transition through the change is critical. Change communications should address the need for change, the impact of the change on stakeholders, the support that will be provided to adjust to the change, and how the change will be reinforced. Addressing change through these communication approaches can help ensure that the organization realizes the intended benefits of the project.

Key Questions

1. Think of the last project you worked on. How was change communicated? What change communications could have been improved?

2. Consider the four change management concepts in the "Communicating Change" section of this chapter. How would you apply them to communications in a current or recent project?

3. Have you ever experienced change fatigue? What were the factors that contributed to it? How were you able to address these factors to overcome change fatigue?

Notes

1. Hamel (2009), https://blogs.wsj.com/management/2009/11/13/outrunning-change-the-cliffsnotes-version-part-ii/.
2. Project Management Institute (2017), *PMBOK® Guide*, 6th ed., p. 6.

3. Hornstein (2015), p. 291.
4. Project Management Institute (2012), *Driving Success in Challenging Times.*
5. Towers Watson (2012), p. 3.
6. Association of Change Management Professionals (2018), p. 9.
7. Association of Change Management Professionals (2018), p. 9.
8. Association of Change Management Professionals (2018), p. 15.
9. Kotter International. https://www.kotterinc.com/8-steps-process-for-leading-change/
10. Cummings and Worley (2008), p. 23–24.
11. Prosci, Inc.
12. Aguirre, et al. (2013) https://www.strategyand.pwc.com/report/cultures-role-organizational-change
13. Project Management Institute (2013), *Managing Change in Organizations: A Practice Guide*, p. 92.

References

Aguirre, D., R. von Post, and M. Alpern. November 14, 2013. "Culture's Role in Enabling Organizational Change." https://www.strategyand.pwc.com/report/cultures-role-organizational-change.

Association of Change Management Professionals. 2018. "Standard for Change Management." Winter Springs, FL: Association of Change Management Professionals.

Creasy, T. 2019. "Adapting and Adjusting Change Management in an Agile Project." *Prosci, Inc.* https://blog.prosci.com/adapting-and-adjusting-change-management-in-agile, (accessed September 2, 2019).

Cummings, T. G. and C. G. Worley. 2008. *Organization Development and Change.* Stamford, CT: Cengage Learning.

Elving, W. J. L. 2005. "The Role of Communication in Organisational Change." *Corporate Communications: An International Journal*, 10, no. 2, pp. 129–138, doi:10.1108/13563280510596943.

Ewenstein, B., W. Smith, and A. Sologar. July, 2015. "Changing Change Management." McKinsey & Company, https://www.mckinsey.com/featured-insights/leadership/changing-change-management.

Hamel, G. November 13, 2009. "Outrunning Change the Cliffs-Notes Version, Part II." *The Wall Street Journal*, https://blogs.wsj.com/management/2009/11/13/outrunning-change-the-cliffsnotes-version-part-ii/.

Harrington, H. J., and D. Nelson. 2013. *The Sponsor as the Face of Organizational Change*. Newtown Square, PA: Project Management Institute.

Hornstein H. A. 2015. "The Integration of Project Management and Organizational Change Management is Now a Necessity." *International Journal of Project Management*, 33, no. 2, pp. 291–298.

Kotter, J. P. 1996. *Leading Change*. Boston: Harvard Business School Press.

Kotter International. "8-Step Process for Leading Change." https://www.kotterinc.com/8-steps-process-for-leading-change/, (accessed September 8, 2019).

Meinert, D. April 1, 2015. "Executive Briefing How to Combat Change Fatigue." *HR Magazine*, https://www.shrm.org/hr-today/news/hr-magazine/pages/0415-execbrief.aspx

Moss Kanter, R. September 25, 2012. "Ten Reasons People Resist Change." *Harvard Business Review*, https://hbr.org/2012/09/ten-reasons-people-resist-chang.

Project Management Institute. 2012. *Driving Success in Challenging Times*. Newtown Square, PA: Project Management Institute.

Project Management Institute. 2017. *A Guide to the Project Management Body of Knowledge*. 6th ed. Newtown Square, PA: Project Management Institute.

Project Management Institute. 2013. *Managing Change in Organizations: A Practice Guide*. Newtown Square, PA: Project Management Institute.

Prosci, Inc. "The Prosci ADKAR Model: A Goal Oriented Change Management Model to Guide Individual and Organizational Change." www.prosci.com, (accessed June 1, 2019).

Towers Watson. "Clear Direction in a Complex World. How Top Companies Create Clarity, Confidence and Community to Build Sustainable Performance." 2011–2012 Change and Communication ROI Study Report.

CHAPTER 9

Managing Conflict through Communication

Projects are, in their very nature, major sources of emotion.[1]
—Nicholas Clarke, management researcher, and Ranse Howell,
conflict resolution expert

Projects are done by people. When there are people involved, there are emotions. Emotions readily lead to conflict. This means that conflict is likely to occur in almost every project, especially when stakes are high, resources are thin, budgets are tight, and time is limited. As your stakeholder analysis should reveal, everyone involved in the project has something at stake (see Chapter 3). When those interests contradict one another or are put in jeopardy (either in a real or perceived way), conflict occurs.

Unresolved conflict can be one of the biggest challenges a project team faces. It can lead to stress, negative attitudes, decreased commitment to the project, and ultimately project failure. Conflict resolution is therefore a critical project management skill—and a critical communication skill. It requires sensitivity, knowledge, and the ability to resolve the conflict in a timely, effective manner that enables the project to continue moving forward smoothly. This chapter offers conflict management strategies that build upon the project communication concepts already introduced in this book.

The purpose of this chapter is to help you:

- Examine two different types of conflict and how they can affect the project and the team
- Explore strategies for understanding and resolving conflict within the project team

- Consider ways to communicate with stakeholders when they do not support the project, when their expectations conflict with one another, or when the project deviates from the plan
- Put it into practice: Managing conflict through communication in traditional, agile, and virtual project teams

Sources of Conflict

Conflicts generally fall into one of two categories: interpersonal conflict and task conflict.[2] These two sources of conflict are parallel to the two types of needs—personal and practical—that should be addressed when managing conversations, as discussed in Chapter 6. Interpersonal and task conflict have different origins, and can affect the team differently. Being able to identify which type of conflict you are facing can help you decide whether to intercede directly, and what to focus on if you do. Remember, however, that both types of conflict need resolution and effective communication. Further, a conflict that starts as one type can evolve into both types, especially when left unchecked.[3]

Interpersonal conflict, also referred to as relational or relationship conflict, arises from incompatibilities among team members based on individual factors like personality, values, background, behavior, or communication style. The team is a social structure made up of individuals working together, and it functions most effectively when all team members feel like they belong and are working toward a common goal. When interpersonal conflict occurs, it can impact the involved team members' sense of team identity. They become uncertain about their place within the team and may start to withdraw, thereby undermining group efforts to get the project done. The conflict can also have negative effects on members of the team who are not directly involved.

Interpersonal conflict can be the most damaging kind of conflict. It takes time and effort to build relationships that result in optimal team functioning. However, conflict can damage those relationships very quickly. Once they are damaged, the relationships can take even more time and work to repair. According to research, it can take up to five positive interactions to overcome the damage of one negative interaction.[4]

Task conflict happens when team members have different perspectives on how to approach the work to be done. This can involve disagreements about distribution of resources, how tasks should be accomplished, or different interpretations of information. Task conflict occurs because team members come to the project from different personal and professional backgrounds, different units within the organization that have their own culture and approach to tasks, and/or different levels of project experience and expertise. These different influences lead team members to think about and approach tasks in different ways.

When people talk about conflict being good for teams, they generally mean task conflict. Different viewpoints and a wide range of experiences can reveal better ways to approach tasks that result in increased efficiencies in the project. This can lead to learning, creativity, and more flexibility in thinking.[5] An example of this is when two project team members disagree on which process or method should be used to complete a project task. To make this conflict productive, the project manager can have the two team members present the pros and cons of their preferred solutions. This can help all team members better understand the implications of each choice and come to a well-informed decision; it can also improve team members' communication skills and demonstrate the value of remaining open to new ideas.[6]

Table 9.1 provides an overview of the two types of conflict, their sources, and their effects on the project team.

Table 9.1 Interpersonal and task conflict

Type of conflict	Sources	Effects
Interpersonal conflict	• Source is unrelated to the team's task • Emotional in nature • Arises from personal dislike, annoyance, personality incompatibility	Negative: Can lead to decline in performance and productivity, withdrawal from collaboration, departure from the team, project failure
Task conflict	• Source is related to the team's task • Cognitive in nature • Arises from difference in perspective	Positive: Can lead to creativity, new solutions, more flexibility in thinking Negative: Can escalate and/or evolve into interpersonal conflict if unresolved

Keep in mind, however, that there is a limit to the benefits of conflict. A review of research on both task and interpersonal conflict found that "whereas a little conflict may be beneficial, such positive effects quickly break down as conflict becomes more intense, cognitive load increases, information processing is impeded, and team performance suffers."[7] Thus, even productive conflict must be managed in order to maintain team cohesiveness and keep the project running smoothly.

Conflict within the Project Team

Effective conflict management has been shown to enhance team performance. Teams that are able to resolve conflict are more cohesive,[8] and cohesion positively impacts perceived performance, satisfaction, and team viability.[9]

On the other hand, unresolved conflict can lead to team members' dissatisfaction, decreased motivation and performance, frustration, anxiety, and even departure from the team.[10,11] It can affect the project through misunderstandings about responsibilities, missed deadlines, lack of collaboration and decreased communication between team members, and unidentified inefficiencies that may result in the project exceeding its schedule and budget.[12]

The first step of managing conflict within the project team is knowing when to get involved. This can be a delicate balance for the project manager, who is responsible for the project and for leading the team, but most likely does not have functional authority over project team members. You should consider interceding if:

- you believe the conflict is having or will have a negative effect on the project,
- the conflict involves you directly, or
- anyone involved in the conflict comes to you for advice or help.

Carefully weigh whether you should involve other organizational resources. If the conflict involves a team member's responsibilities on the project interfering with their other functional responsibilities, it may be prudent to communicate with or involve the individual's functional manager. If the conflict is interpersonal and highly emotional, you may want to consult human resources before proceeding.

When you do step in to help manage conflict, remember this basic rule: Focus on the project or the problem, not the person! While there are a number of conflict resolution strategies and approaches available, many involve some aspect of the following three steps: de-escalate, redirect, and exit.[13] You may recognize aspects of the five-step approach to managing conversations we introduced in Chapter 6. Note that this approach can be applied whether you are involved in the conflict directly, or are mediating a conflict between others.

> Focus on the project or the problem, not the person!

Step 1: De-escalate

Managing emotions is particularly difficult in conflict—these situations can elicit physiological responses that are difficult to control, such as increased heart rate, sweating palms, or tensing muscles. These are symptoms of the fight-or-flight response, and they happen because the subconscious mind can interpret conflict as a threat. They also interfere with the part of the brain that controls rational thinking. As a result, individuals in conflict may raise their voices or bring up unrelated or unproductive issues in an attempt to attack the other person. This pattern of communication and behavior does not resolve the conflict, and ends up damaging relationships between team members.

De-escalating the conversation is an effort to avoid additional damage to the team members' relationships. As noted earlier in this chapter, damaged interpersonal relationships can be difficult to repair, and can have a detrimental effect on the project. Remind involved parties that, "The person in front of you is more important than the feeling inside of you."[14] Ask them to focus their words on the situation at hand, rather than on any personal comments, attacks, or blame.

Take a break if necessary, especially if emotions are high. Stopping for a few minutes can give everyone a chance to process their emotions, and allow physiological fight-or-flight responses to diminish. Call for a break—to get a drink of water, use the restroom, or get some fresh air—and give everyone an opportunity to come back to the conversation with clearer heads.

Step 2: Redirect

Bring the conversation back to the issue at hand. Intensified conversation (e.g., raised voices, unproductive criticisms or insults, etc.) is not the same as important communication—the intensity becomes what's important instead of the source of the conflict.

First, clarify the facts. Some conflict can be resolved simply by giving both sides the full picture of what happened. Next, clarify intent. People often make assumptions about intent; they assign specific intentions to another person's words or actions.[15] For example, "He e-mailed you about my work being late because he was trying to undermine me and make himself look good at my expense." Give each party the opportunity to explain their intent to dispel any assumptions. Conflict, after all, often arises from uncertainties; by helping to reduce or manage these uncertainties, you can reduce or manage the conflict they have sparked.

Skip the blame and focus on the outcome. Clearly communicate that your goal is to resolve the conflict in a way that allows the entire team to move forward together to accomplish the project objective. In conflict, people frequently get hung up on the idea of assigning blame. For example, "This deliverable is late because she didn't get to me report on time." In general, people do not like to acknowledge that they have done something wrong and are at fault or partially at fault. They are uncertain about the consequences, fearing negative repercussions that range from being viewed as incompetent, to losing their job.[16] Make it clear what the consequences are, if any; this will reduce uncertainty and allow those involved to move forward in the resolution process. Then, work on the outcome with input from all parties, which should focus on compensating for any problems or issues that have affected the project, and putting mechanisms in place to attempt to prevent the issue from occurring again.

Step 3: Exit

Once a resolution has been found, make sure both parties accept it. Give each of them an opportunity to communicate any additional thoughts or concerns, so that you can be sure the conflict is truly resolved. If the situation has impacted the project, make the necessary updates to the project plan, schedule, or other project documents. If appropriate, add it to your lessons learned document as well.

If you are unable to come to a satisfactory resolution, ask the involved parties to table the issue for now. This gives you the opportunity to step back from the conflict and consider more potential solutions. You may want to call upon additional resources such as functional managers, subject matter experts, human resources personnel, the client or sponsor, or other stakeholders for input on the best way to resolve the issue. Be sure to set a time to reconvene, so that everyone has a clear expectation about when the issue will be addressed again.

Conflict resolution can be very challenging. It is not an easy skill to develop, and often requires individuals to engage in difficult conversations. It is, however, an important skill for project managers and team members. As we stated at the beginning of this chapter, unresolved team conflict can be one of the biggest challenges a project team faces. Resolved conflict, meanwhile, carries benefits beyond renewed smooth progress on the project. Successful conflict resolution can also help build team cohesion and trust, more so than if conflict had never occurred in the first place.[17]

QTIP

We often struggle with conflict because it can impact how we see ourselves. Someone may criticize a specific task—for example, a project report that missed a key piece of information—and we subconsciously generalize it to be a critique of who we are: "I am incompetent." We take the situation personally, which makes it far more difficult to resolve the conflict.[18]

One simple, visual tool that can help you and your project team remember to fight this tendency is a cotton swab, known in the U.S. by its brand name, Q-tip®. This brand name is also an acronym for **Quit Taking It Personally**. Early in the project, set aside a few minutes to relay this advice and hand out cotton swabs to everyone on the team. Ask them to keep their cotton swabs somewhere visible as a reminder of this important lesson—don't take it personally, focus on the project.

Managing Conflict with Stakeholders outside the Project

As we've seen so far in this chapter, managing conflict within the project team involves direct conflict management approaches and skilled communication. The goal is to preserve team cohesion and come to an agreement on the best way to resolve the conflict so that the team can move forward in achieving the project objectives. However, conflict *outside* the project team can materialize in very different ways that may require different approaches. Here are three common scenarios where you must work through conflict with stakeholders outside of the project team:

1. Working with stakeholders who are resistant to the project
2. Communicating project setbacks to stakeholders
3. Handling conflict between project stakeholders

When Stakeholders Do Not Support the Project

Many projects, especially those that can significantly disrupt "business as usual," will likely have stakeholders who do not support the project. In Chapter 3, we examined the spectrum of stakeholder support, from unaware or resistant to supportive or leading. Those on the resistant side of the spectrum may say or do things to weaken support for, or even interfere with, the project. The *PMBOK® Guide* addresses this issue under the process of Manage Stakeholder Engagement, part of the Project Stakeholder Management Knowledge Area. "The key benefit of this process is that it allows the project manager to increase support and minimize resistance from stakeholders."[19]

Once you identify stakeholders who may be resistant to your project, the following recommendations may help minimize their resistance, reduce the likelihood of conflict or its intensity when it arises, and even move them toward being more supportive of the project:

Communicate early and frequently. Keep resistant stakeholders in the loop. This can help build trust by demonstrating that you understand and respect their interest and/or impact on the project, and want to engage with them despite their disposition toward the project. Build these communications into your project communications management plan.

Seek feedback regularly. Check in with these stakeholders either with a set frequency (e.g. monthly) or at project milestones. Encourage honest feedback, and provide direct responses to their concerns to the greatest extent possible. (See Chapter 6 for more on seeking feedback.) Don't forget to refer back to your stakeholder analysis and project communications management plan when communicating with stakeholders.

Get the stakeholder involved. If the stakeholder is particularly resistant, or if you are not successfully able to address their concerns on your own, engage them in working with you toward a solution. Get their input on what it will take to reduce or resolve their resistance to the project, and then ask them to help in putting that solution into practice.

Give these strategies a try, and make the necessary adjustments when needed.

Giving Stakeholders Bad News

Another stakeholder situation that may involve conflict is having to communicate bad news to key stakeholders who have a high level of interest and/or investment in the project. For example, a problem may materialize that results in project work needing to be done over, causing a delay in the project schedule. How do you communicate this news that key stakeholders may not want to hear, and may react poorly to? What you say is important, but so is when and how you say it.

> What you say is important, but so is when and how you say it.

Here are some recommendations on how to conduct these difficult conversations.

What: Focus on what happened, how it impacts the project—cost, schedule, scope, etc.—and how it is going to be corrected and prevented moving forward. Give a clear explanation of the problem and why it occurred. Do not focus on who is at fault; instead, focus on how you plan to fix the problem and/or prevent it from recurring, and how you will minimize the negative impact on the project. Some of this may already be addressed in your risk management planning.

When: The higher the stakes, the sooner you should tell the stakeholder(s). In some cases, immediate action can help mitigate the effects of the problem. As soon as you understand the source and impacts of the issue and have identified a plan of corrective action, talk to the stakeholder. If you are not able to propose corrective action immediately, you will still want to inform the stakeholder and ask for their support in developing a solution.

How: Negative news should be delivered in person, or at least through a real-time, two-way channel such as a telephone call or video call. This can be intimidating because the stakeholder may not react well to the news, regardless of how supportive of the project they may be. Despite this possibility, do not use an asynchronous communication channel like e-mail or text. Real-time conversations allow the stakeholder to ask questions, show them that you are accountable for the project, and help preserve trust and relationships despite the problem at hand.

The conflict resolution steps noted above can be useful to help navigate difficult conversations like these. If the stakeholder does react poorly, focus first on de-escalating the interaction. Keep the focus on resolving the issue and honestly answering the stakeholder's questions. When you conclude the conversation, reinforce your commitment to correcting the action, and affirm the stakeholder's buy-in to the solution and the project as a whole.

Once the issue is addressed, don't forget the follow-up. Continue to keep affected stakeholders apprised with updates on the proposed solution and its effectiveness. This can be done through ad hoc communications when necessary, or within planned communication methods like status reports. Finally, identify and document the lessons learned. This will benefit you, the project, and the project team going forward to prevent or mitigate similar issues from affecting this project as well as future projects. And don't forget to update your project communications management plan as needed.

Managing Conflict between Stakeholders

Stakeholders have different expectations and priorities for projects—this is the "what's in it for me", or WIIFM concept that we discussed in Chapter 3. The sponsor may be most concerned about the project staying within budget, while operational groups who will use the results of the project may be most concerned about the project finishing on time. Sometimes, it may not be possible to meet both stakeholders' expectations completely. Conflict may result that can jeopardize the project's progress and potential for success.

Interpersonal conflict can also occur between stakeholders, just as it can occur among members of the project team. Potential areas for interpersonal conflict can be identified as you conduct a thorough analysis of your stakeholder audience, including role, power and influence, level of support, and priorities and expectations. This is also an area where expert judgment can be useful. As noted in the Project Stakeholder Management Knowledge Area of the *PMBOK® Guide*, expert judgment can identify considerations around political and power structures in the organization and among stakeholders, organizational culture and environment, and knowledge from past projects and stakeholder interactions that may influence the current project. Finally, when talking with stakeholder groups, listen closely for any clues that may indicate conflict with other stakeholders. A member of the executive team may remark that he has had a past negative experience with a resource manager or a vendor. Note these potential issues so that you can be on the lookout for conflicts that may arise.

As you identify stakeholder priorities and document them in your stakeholder register, spend some time reviewing where expectations or personalities may conflict. Depending on the size and complexity of your project, you may want to ask the project team to contribute to this exercise as well. A simple tool like the stakeholder conflict template in Table 9.2 may help.

If conflict occurs between stakeholders, address it early to prevent it from escalating and putting the project at risk. Communication approaches such as the five-step technique for managing conversations outlined in Chapter 6, or the more basic three-step approach to addressing conflict noted earlier in this chapter, may be sufficient to mitigate the conflict. However, because project managers and team members have no functional authority over most stakeholders, seeking support from other organizational resources such as project leadership, senior management, or human resources may be necessary.

In any given project, there's a good chance something will not go according to plan. Sometimes these are identified risks that materialize, and

Table 9.2 Stakeholder conflict template example

	Stakeholder 1	Stakeholder 2	Stakeholder 3
Stakeholder 1		Budget (stakeholder 1) could conflict with scope (stakeholder 2)	
Stakeholder 2			Past negative interactions between stakeholders 2 and 3
Stakeholder 3	Schedule (stakeholder 3) could conflict with resources (stakeholder 1)		

sometimes they are unexpected. No matter what the issue, conflict can result. Using effective communication strategies like those discussed in this chapter can have a major impact on how the conflict affects the project, and on your reputation and effectiveness as a project manager. Remember: It's not about whether things go wrong, it's about how you handle them when they do.

Putting It into Practice

Here are a few practical tips, fun activities, and useful ideas for how you can implement the concepts in this chapter into your project environment. Note that ideas listed in one type of team may be adapted to other teams. Be creative. Use these as a starting point. Add your own ideas to build your communications toolkit.

Managing conflict through communication	
Traditional project teams	• At the end of an intense discussion or meeting, ask each participant to share something positive about themselves—or someone else on the team. • Encourage/reward conflict that is handled appropriately. Look for opportunities to positively acknowledge team members who do so. • At the beginning of the project, send a brief survey to each team member asking them how they feel about conflict. Use the results (without revealing names) to facilitate a discussion on how you expect conflict to be handled on the project. Add the discussion outcome to your team operating principles. (This is a good time to introduce the QTIP lesson.)

Agile project teams	• Effectively utilize an agile coach (or agile mentor) to help agile team members deal with conflict. An agile coach who is experienced in people skills and agile practices and processes can help team members through challenging times and situations. • When conflict occurs, look for the root cause and address it quickly. Otherwise, it will slow down the rapid progress and results that agile teams desire. • Encourage servant leadership of coaching, mentoring, collaborating, communicating, and helping others. This is the best way to reduce conflict and keep the team moving forward.
Virtual project teams	• Virtual teams often exhibit more cultural diversity, as team members may be spread across the globe. Ask each team member to share something about their culture with the group. • When you do hold in-person meetings with virtual teams, be sure to incorporate some hands-on team-building activities. The project may seem like the priority, but that can be done virtually. Use face-to-face time to build relationships and trust among the team. • Conflict creates tension and can multiply rapidly when not properly or quickly addressed. When conflict occurs, it may be necessary to travel and meet with the stakeholder or team member(s) in person. This shows your attentiveness to the situation and willingness to achieve resolution so that the project and team can succeed.

Summary

Since projects are done by people, conflict is likely to occur. This is where your communication skills are most needed to effectively manage conflict within the project team and among stakeholders outside the team. There are two sources of conflict: interpersonal conflict (relational conflict) and task conflict (objective disagreements). Task conflict can be a good thing. Positive conflict can be the foundation for stronger relationships and greater results. Interpersonal conflict and unresolved task conflict, however, can have negative effects on the project and the team.

Project professionals handle and manage conflict through various communication strategies. Handling conflict within the project team requires knowing when to intercede, and how to address the situation when you do. Project teams who are able to resolve conflict quickly and effectively are more cohesive and achieve greater results than those teams who let conflict go unresolved, hindering project and team success.

Conflict with stakeholders outside the project team can occur when stakeholders are unsupportive of the project, when you must communicate problems or delays in the project to the stakeholder, or when two different stakeholders have conflicting expectations or personalities. Respond to these situations quickly, honestly, and with support from organizational resources when necessary.

When addressing conflict, you may find some strategies work, and other approaches need to be modified, based on the situation and people involved. Make the necessary adjustments in your communications—with the goal of conflict resolution. And don't forget the QTIP: Quit Taking It Personally.

Key Questions

1. Think back on your project experiences where conflict has occurred. Was it task conflict or interpersonal conflict? How was it handled? If it occurred again, what would you suggest be done differently?

2. When you have experienced conflict on a project team, what communication strategies have you used? What adjustments to these strategies have you made?

3. What benefits have you experienced or seen from positive conflict on a team? What challenges have you experienced or seen when conflict goes unresolved?

Notes

1. Clarke and Howell (2009), p. 4.
2. Chen (2006), p. 107.
3. Chen (2006), p. 111.
4. Tumlin (2013), p 50.
5. Chen (2006), p.107.
6. Estafanous, 2018.
7. De Dreu and Weingart (2003), p. 746.
8. Nesterkin and Porterfield (2016), p 15.
9. Tekleab, et al. (2009), p. 194.
10. Jehn (1994).
11. De Dreu and Weingart (2003).
12. Susskind and Odom-Reed (2019).
13. Tumlin (2013), p. 67.

14. Tumlin (2013), p. 62.

15. Stone, et al. (2010), p. 11.

16. Stone, et al. (2010), p 12.

17. Tekleab, et al. (2009), p. 171.

18. Stone, et al. (2010), p. 14.

19. Project Management Institute (2017), *PMBOK® Guide*, 6th ed., p. 523.

References

Alexander, M. July 1, 2015. "7 Tips to Transform Difficult Stakeholders into Project Partners." *CIO*, https://www.cio.com/article/2942210/7-tips-to-transform-difficult-stakeholders-into-project-partners.html.

Alexander, M. December 29, 2016. "8 Steps to Breaking Bad News to Difficult Project Stakeholders." *TechRepublic*, https://www.techrepublic.com/article/8-steps-to-breaking-bad-news-to-difficult-project-stakeholders/.

Chen, M. H. 2006. "Understanding the Benefits and Detriments of Conflict on Team Creativity Process." *Creativity and Innovation Management* 15, no. 1, pp. 105–116.

Clarke, N. and R. Howell. 2009. *Emotional Intelligence and Projects.* Newtown Square, PA: Project Management Institute.

De Dreu, Carsten K. W., and L. R. Weingart. 2003. "Task Versus Relationship Conflict, Team Performance, and Team Member Satisfaction: A Meta-Analysis." *Journal of Applied Psychology* 88, no. 4, pp. 741–749.

Estafanous, J. October 27, 2018. "Why Your Team Needs Conflict and How to Make it Productive." *The Startup, a Medium Corporation.* https://medium.com/swlh/why-your-team-needs-conflict-and-how-to-make-it-productive-8475da62282c, (accessed September 7, 2019).

Gallo, A. December 1, 2017. "How to Control Your Emotions During a Difficult Conversation," *Harvard Business Review*, https://hbr.org/2017/12/how-to-control-your-emotions-during-a-difficult-conversation.

Jehn, K. A. 1994. "Enhancing Effectiveness an Investigation of Advantages and Disadvantages of Valuebased Intragroup Conflict." *International Journal of Conflict Management* 5, no. 3, pp. 223–238.

Krumrie, M. 2019. "How and When to Manage Conflict." Monster.com, https://www.monster.com/career-advice/article/managing-conflict-how-and-when, (accessed September 7, 2019).

Lalegani, Z., A. N. Isfahani, A. Shahin, and A. Safari. 2019. "Developing a Model for Analyzing the Factors Influencing Interpersonal Conflict." *Management Decision* 57, no. 5, pp. 1127–1144.

Lee, S., S. Kwon, S. J. Shin, M. Kim, and I.-J. Park. 2018. "How Team-Level Conflict Influences Team Commitment: A Multilevel Investigation." *Frontiers in Psychology*, 8, pp 1–13.

Nesterkin, D., and T. Porterfield. 2016. "Conflict Management and Performance of Information Technology Development Teams." *Team Performance Management* 22, no. 5/6, pp. 242–256.

Porter, T. W., and B. S. Lilly. 1996. "The Effects of Conflict, Trust, and Task Commitment on Project Team Performance." *International Journal of Conflict Management* 7, no. 4, pp. 361–376.

Project Management Institute. 2017. *A Guide to the Project Management Body of Knowledge.* 6th ed. Newtown Square, PA: Project Management Institute.

Semeniuk, M. February 24, 2010. "Running with Scissors: Techniques for Managing Conflicting Expectations." Paper presented at PMI® Global Congress 2010—Asia Pacific, Melbourne, Victoria, Australia, https://www.pmi.org/learning/library/managing-conflicting-expectations-6893.

Stone, D., B. Patton and S. Heen. 2010. *Difficult Conversations: How to Discuss What Matters Most.* 10th anniversary ed. New York, NY: Penguin Group.

Susskind, A. M., and P. R. Odom-Reed. 2019. "Team Member's Centrality, Cohesion, Conflict, and Performance in Multi-University Geographically Distributed Project Teams." *Communication Research* 46, no. 2, pp. 151–178.

Tekleab, A. G., N. R. Quigley, and P. E. Tesluk. 2009. "A Longitudinal Study of Team Conflict, Conflict Management, Cohesion, and Team Effectiveness." *Group & Organization Management: An International Journal* 34, no. 2, pp. 170–205.

Tumlin, G. 2013. *Stop Talking, Start Communicating.* New York, NY: McGraw-Hill Education.

Villax, C., and V. S. Anantatmula. July 14, 2010. "Understanding and Managing Conflict in a Project Environment." Paper presented at PMI® Research Conference: Defining the Future of Project Management, Washington, DC, https://www.pmi.org/learning/library/understanding-managing-conflict-resolution-strategies-6484

CHAPTER 10

Closing

Ends are not bad things; they just mean that something else is about to begin. And there are many things that don't really end, anyway, they just begin again in a new way. Ends are not bad, and many ends aren't really an ending; some things are never-ending.

—C. JoyBell C., author[1]

As this quote states, "some things are never-ending," which is true when it comes to growing your skills as an effective communicator on projects. There is always something to learn. There is always a new approach, a new technique to try. As project professionals, we keep developing ourselves. We keep growing our experiences, skills, and knowledge, and transforming our talents into strengths. We are dedicated to being continuous, lifelong learners.

Learning, practicing, and improving our project communications to be more effective is never-ending. For some, the communications journey may just be beginning. For others, the journey may be well on its way. Consider this book to be the tip of the iceberg on the topic of project communications. There is so much more that could be written and shared about communicating on projects—emotional intelligence, human behavior, leadership traits, diverse cultures, and different languages, just to name a few. The intent of this book is to provide you with the *essentials* in good project communications, from the evolution, to foundational concepts, to various theories, practices, and tools, and to the bigger picture when it comes to effective project communications.

The purpose of this final chapter is to help you:

- See where we have been and where we are going from here
- Know how to put this information into a personalized action plan
- Explore different ways to communicate the value of project management

A Time to Reflect

Just like lessons learned, retrospectives, or project evaluations, it is important to pause and reflect on where we have been.

In the beginning, we traveled through time and looked at the evolution of project communications through the lens of the *PMBOK® Guide*. Why is this important? Because the *PMBOK® Guide* is written by project management practitioners from around the world and shows us how project communications (and project management knowledge) have progressed, not just from an individual perspective but from a global view. Refer to the evolution of project communications as you continue to evolve your own project communications (see Chapter 1).

To build a solid foundation for project communications and have a better appreciation of uncertainty, we explored two communication theories—uncertainty reduction theory and uncertainty management theory. Why is this important? Because *understanding* uncertainty as a motivator can help project managers and stakeholders appreciate the value of communication as a way to *manage* uncertainty. There are two ways to reduce uncertainty: to ensure sufficient quantity and high-quality communications. Focus on building trust among the project team and other stakeholders—a key factor in project success (see Chapter 2).

We examined the importance of knowing your audience and how different factors can affect stakeholders' engagement with your communications. Start with the WIIFM—what's in it for me. Developing stakeholder personas can help capture stakeholders' characteristics and concerns as a group. Why is this important? By knowing your audience, you can tailor your communications for them, leading to decreased uncertainty, increased trust, and a greater possibility of project support and success (see Chapter 3).

It is important to start with the basics in project communications. We looked at how high-performing organizations and project teams are more effective at project communications than others. We explored some practical and sensible approaches for effectively delivering your message when communicating on projects. Why is this important? Because it may stimulate new ideas for you to explore or reconfirm effective approaches that may already be working well for you. Make every word and interaction meaningful (see Chapter 4).

In any project, it is important to have a plan; so is having a project communications management plan—and using it. A project communications management plan and its various elements provide a roadmap for the project team to keep others informed. Make sure your plan is being used effectively. As the project team implements their project communications management plan, the team may find that adjustments are needed. Why is this important? Because a project communications management plan and its evolution help us to stay on track by delivering the right message, at the right time, to the right stakeholders, for the right reasons, using the right communication methods and frequency (see Chapter 5).

Once you have planned your project communications, you are now ready to start using your project communications management plan through managing and monitoring project communications. Don't forget to measure the effectiveness of your project communications. Ask questions like, "What do you think?" or "What did you just hear?" Why is this important? Getting and giving feedback, having structured conversations, and addressing the personal and practical needs of the project team and stakeholders are all essential in managing and monitoring project communications (see Chapter 6).

We explored different communication tools and how to select the best tools that fit your project needs and organization by starting with *why*, then *how*, then *what*. Establishing the priorities of your selection criteria can help you focus on *what matters most*. Selecting the right tool is as important as knowing how to use the tool. If you need education in how to use a tool, get it. If you need to change the tool because it is not working, do it. Why is this important? Because tools are vital in communicating. In projects, we use a collection of tools when communicating. Even our talents and strengths are a tool. However, remember that our primary focus is on the message and the communication. Consider the communication tool as the vehicle for delivering the message (see Chapter 7).

Projects are the connectors between where we are now (current state) and where we want to be (future state). In the middle, there is change and uncertainty. There are a number of change management models to consider for integrating change management concepts into your project communications. Be cautious, however, that too much change can create change fatigue, which can put projects and teams at risk. Why is this important? Because effective project communications that incorporate change management principles can help projects succeed and help organizations realize the benefits of the project (see Chapter 8).

And finally, things happen. We looked at how to effectively communicate when conflict occurs on the project. There are two sources of conflict: interpersonal conflict (relational conflict) and task conflict (disagreements). A moderate amount of conflict can have a positive outcome by building stronger relationships and generating better project results. Too much conflict can have a negative outcome, causing dysfunctional project teams, unhappy stakeholders, and poor project results. Why is this important? Because like other problem-solving situations, we must address conflict with different strategies—using what works and/or adjusting when the approach does not work. Bottom line: Don't take it personally (see Chapter 9).

In closing, we need to put it into practice. Communication is vital for all project teams, regardless of the type of team, the type of project management methodology, or the type of project. The tips and ideas presented in the "putting it into practice" sections at the end of Chapters 3 to 9 are intended to stimulate your thinking on additional ways to put these concepts into action—which is our next topic.

A Time to Look Forward—and Take Action

Now that you have read this book on project communications, what's next? Too often we read a book, listen to a webinar, or attend a training class, and do nothing with the information that we have gained. Or sometimes we ask ourselves: "There is so much here. Where do I start?" Everyone has a different starting point. Just like projects address different needs, everyone has different needs in building their project communication skills. We suggest you choose where to start based on what content or ideas resonate the most with you.

Don't try to implement everything at once. Pick one or two things that have the greatest relevance for you, and start there. It is better to implement one or two small tweaks to your project communications, than to try to do it all and wind up doing none of it well. Follow the same steps you would in building any new habit—start small, celebrate mini-successes, and slowly continue to build on your progress over time.

Another technique to use in getting started is to sum it up. Using the S.U.M. technique, write down one or two key learnings that you have gained by reading this book.

S = What was surprising?

U = What was useful?

M = What was memorable?

Use your answers to these three questions to jumpstart the creation of your own action plan. Creating (and following) an action plan will help you use and improve your project communications. An action plan is designed to be personal. As mentioned in Chapter 1, it is not "one size fits all." Design your action plan to fit your needs. Your action plan will be different from another team member's action plan, and may be different from one project to the next. Where should you start? If you need help, here is a template to consider using as a framework (Table 10.1). Note: It is intended that you modify this template to fit your needs.

Table 10.1 Action plan template

Skill to work on	Steps to implement	Due date	Chapters to review	What does success look like?	Done √

- Skill to work on: Describe the skill that needs development or improvement. Be specific.
- Steps to implement: List the activities you will do that are relevant to improving the skill you seek to improve.
- Due date: Establish a specific date by which you plan to complete each step.
- Chapters to review: Refer to the various sections in this book as reference points and for ideas to implement.
- What does success look like: Describe how you will know you have completed development of the specific skill.
- Done: Use a checkmark to show completion. Celebrate your success. However, don't forget that you need to keep practicing this skill for greater improvement. Then add a new skill to the action plan that you will start working on next.

As you create your action plan, consider reviewing the key questions at the end of each chapter (and in Appendix D) to generate ideas for skills to work on—for your own professional development or coursework for school. Sometimes it can be difficult to hold yourself accountable to follow and complete your action plan. Therefore, consider asking a colleague, team member, or another student to help you be accountable for implementing your action plan and practicing/experiencing the improvements. Your action plan will provide a roadmap for improving your project communication skills, knowledge, techniques, relationships, and, ultimately, project results.

Communicating the Value of Project Management

There is one final area where good communication skills will serve you well as a project professional—in communicating what project management is and the value it can provide. Not every stakeholder knows or understands what project management is. In fact, for some, your project may be their first. Therefore, it is necessary to take the time to share with them what project management is, why it is important, and what your role is in leading or supporting the project to successful completion. Exhibit 10.1 provides a list of "value points" that may be helpful: different ways you can explain the value of project management to your stakeholders. This list is not inclusive of all value points. Rather, it provides a foundation you can build on in your project communications.

Exhibit 10.1

Project management value points

- **Save time, money, and resources.** "When project managers employ standardized processes and proven techniques, projects are typically completed more quickly, saving money, time, and resources."[2]
- **Drive measurable results.** "PMPs® and other certified project professionals have the technical project management skills, leadership capabilities, strategic mindset, communication, and team-building skills needed to drive measurable results."[3]

- **Deliver benefits.** "Investment in effective project management will have a number of benefits, such as:
  - providing a greater likelihood of achieving the desired result;
  - ensuring efficient and best value use of resources;
  - satisfying the differing needs of the project's stakeholders."[4]
- **Achieve the goal.** "Through proper project management, you can assure that the purpose/vision and goals of the project are maintained, all while supporting the audiences' tasks and objectives. Additionally, you avoid risks and effectively and efficiently use your available resources. It also helps the team members to understand their responsibilities, the deliverables expected, and the schedule everyone needs to follow to complete the project on time and within budget."[5]

In being an effective project communicator, you are role modeling not just good communication, but good project management. Communicating effectively with stakeholders inside and outside the project team will build their trust and reduce their uncertainty, both in you and in the role—as a project manager, team member, or project sponsor. Remember that you are representing not only yourself and your organization, but your profession.

Summary

As reflected in the studies and research presented throughout this book, organizations know effective communications are key to project success. Stakeholders know it. The project team knows it. Which brings us back to a key question we asked at the end of Chapter 1: "If so much has been written about effective communication in projects, why does ineffective communication continue, risking project success?" Hopefully you now have a better understanding of specific project communication concepts and tools that you can put into place which will lead to successful projects and avoid the risk of project failure.

Finally, remember that it is up to YOU! As the project participant, you want project success. While there are many factors within a project that you cannot control, how well you communicate with stakeholders is 100 percent within your control. You have a choice: action or inaction. You can take action by continuing to grow your skills and effectiveness as a project communicator. Or you can choose inaction by doing nothing, hoping that things might work out and that team members and stakeholders will somehow get all of the information they need. The choice is yours. However, keep in mind that research and experience demonstrate that communicating effectively through a well-executed project communications management plan and using effective project management tools and techniques will increase the likelihood of project success.

Zig Ziglar, an American motivational speaker and author, once said: "You don't have to be great to start, but you have to start to be great."[6] So start your journey today to become a great project communicator. After all, …

Project communications are a critical factor for project success!

Key Questions

1. Using the S.U.M. technique, write down one or two key learnings for each of the following questions: What information in this book has been most surprising for you (S)? What information has been most useful (U)? What information has been the most memorable (M)? Share your answers with a colleague, team member, student, or professor.

2. Develop your action plan for improving your project communications. What key skills would you include? To get started, list three skills you would like to improve, with at least one actionable step you can take to build each skill. Share your action plan with a colleague and ask for their help in holding you accountable for progress and completion.

Notes

1. Goodreads, C. JoyBell C., https://www.goodreads.com/quotes/ 455537-ends-are-not-bad-things-they-just-mean-that-something.
2. Villanova University, https://www.villanovau.com/resources/project-management/the-value-of-having-a-project-manager/.

3. Alexander, 2018.
4. Association for Project Management, https://www.apm.org.uk/resources/what-is-project-management/.
5. Usability.gov, https://www.usability.gov/what-and-why/project-management.html.
6. Goodreads, Zig Ziglar, https://www.goodreads.com/quotes/59427-you-don-t-have-to-be-great-to-start-but-you.

References

Alexander, M. November, 2018. "The True Value of a Project Management Professional." *TechRepublic*, https://www.techrepublic.com/article/the-true-value-of-a-project-management-professional/, (accessed August 31, 2019).

Association for Project Management. "What is Project Management?" https://www.apm.org.uk/resources/what-is-project-management/, (accessed August 31, 2019).

Usability.gov. "Project Management Basics." https://www.usability.gov/what-and-why/project-management.html, (accessed August 31, 2019).

Villanova University. March 14, 2019. "The Value of Having a Project Manager." https://www.villanovau.com/resources/project-management/the-value-of-having-a-project-manager/.

GoodReads, C. JoyBell C. https://www.goodreads.com/quotes/59427-you-don-t-have-to-be-great-to-start-but-you, (accessed August 31, 2019).

GoodReads, Zig Ziglar. https://www.goodreads.com/quotes/59427-you-don-t-have-to-be-great-to-start-but-you, (accessed September 24, 2019).

APPENDIX A

Evolution of Project Communications

Communication has been considered a project management knowledge area in every version of professional standards published by the Project Management Institute (PMI). As the standards have evolved, the approach to communication has broadened from a process-oriented, information-dissemination function, to a holistic, purposeful means to engage and satisfy stakeholders.

The chart in Figure A.1 provides a high-level overview of the changes in the Project Communications Management Knowledge Area in *A Guide to the Project Management Body of Knowledge* (*PMBOK® Guide*) from the first edition published in 1996 through to the current sixth edition published in 2017.

PMBOK® **Guide** **1st edition** **(1996)**	• Communications is for information dissemination • Differentiation between general communications skills and communications in project management • Expectation for stakeholders to understand project language • Project Communications Management Knowledge Area is 8 pages, includes 4 processes
PMBOK® **Guide** **2nd edition** **(2000)**	• Relatively few changes • Expectation for stakeholders to understand project language is no longer included • Knowledge Area is 10 pages, same 4 processes as 1st edition
PMBOK® **Guide** **3rd edition** **(2004)**	• View of communication begins to broaden, with an emphasis on the importance of meeting the communications needs of stakeholders • Introduces basic communications model of sender–message–receiver • Administrative Closure process removed, Manage Stakeholders process added • Knowledge Area is 16 pages, 4 processes (with changes as noted above)
PMBOK® **Guide** **4th edition** **(2008)**	• Clearly states that project managers spend the majority of their time communicating • Identify Stakeholders process added • Increasing emphasis on stakeholders as partners in ensuring project success • Knowledge Area jumps to 29 pages, 5 processes
PMBOK® **Guide** **5th edition** **(2013)**	• Stakeholder Management separated into its own knowledge area • Knowledge Area decreases to 22 pages, 3 processes: Plan Communications Management, Manage Communications, and Control Communications
PMBOK® **Guide** **6th edition** **(2017)**	• Purpose of communications is ensuring the information needs of stakeholders are met • New concepts are added: Key Concepts, Trends and Emerging Practices, Tailoring Considerations, Considerations for Agile/Adaptive Environments • Knowledge Area jumps to 35 pages, 3 processes (same as 5th edition, with one change: Control Communications is renamed to Monitor Communications)

Figure A.1 An overview of the evolution of the Project Communications Management Knowledge Area in the PMBOK® Guide

For more detailed information, refer to the various editions of the *PMBOK® Guide.*

APPENDIX B

Resource Guide

Listed below are resources for additional information on topics related to project management and communication.

Organizations

Association of Change Management Professionals (ACMP)
—https://www.acmpglobal.org/
Development Dimensions International (DDI)
—www.ddiworld.com
Project Management Institute (PMI)
—www.pmi.org
Prosci
—https://www.prosci.com/
The Association for Business Communication (ABC)
—https://www.businesscommunication.org/

Related Books from Business Expert Press

Developing Strengths-Based Project Teams by Martha Buelt and Connie Plowman

Managing Virtual Teams, (2nd ed.) by Debbie D. Dufrene and Carol M. Lehman

Project Communications from Start to Finish by Geraldine E. Hynes

Project Management Essentials by Timothy J. Kloppenborg and Kathryn N. Wells

Books on Project Management

A Guide to the Project Management Body of Knowledge (PMBOK® Guide) by Project Management Institute

Agile Practice Guide by Project Management Institute

Contemporary Project Management (4th ed.) by Timothy Kloppenborg, Vittal S. Anantatmula, and Kathryn Wells

Emotional Intelligence and Projects by Nicholas Clarke and Ranse Howell

Project Manager Competency Development Framework (3rd ed.) by Project Management Institute

The Complete Project Manager by Randall L. Englund and Alfonso Bucero

The Social Project Manager by Peter Taylor

Books on Leadership

Project Leadership by Timothy J. Kloppenborg, Arthur Shriberg, and Jayashree Venkatraman

Start with Why by Simon Sinek

Your First Leadership Job: How Catalyst Leaders Bring Out the Best in Others by Tacy M. Byham and Richard S. Wellins

Books on Communication, Stakeholders, and Related Topics

Active Listening: Improve Your Ability to Listen and Lead by Center for Creative Leadership (CCL) and Michael H. Hoppe

Communication Skills for Project Managers by Michael Campbell

Crucial Conversations by Kerry Patterson, Joseph Grenny, Ron McMillan, and Al Switzler

Difficult Conversations: How to Discuss What Matters Most by Douglas Stone, Bruce Patton, and Sheila Heen

Managing Project Stakeholders by Tres Roeder

Managing Stakeholders as Clients by Mario Henrique Trentim

Project Management Communication Tools by William Dow and Bruce Taylor

Reinventing Communication: How to Design, Lead and Manage High Performing Projects by Mark Phillip

Rethink! Project Stakeholder Management by Martina Huemann, Pernille Eskerod, and Claudia Ringhofer

Stop Talking Start Communicating by Geoffrey Tumlin

The High Cost of Low Performance: The Essential Role of Communications by Project Management Institute

APPENDIX C

Templates

This is a consolidation of the various templates that have been presented throughout the book.

Chapter 3

Stakeholder register template

Stakeholder	Role	Power	Influence	Support	WIIFM
Stakeholder 1					
Stakeholder 2					
Stakeholder 3					

Stakeholder persona template

Stakeholder name:		
Characteristics	Organizational role Role within the project Reporting structure	
Support	Current level of support Desired level of support	
Motivations	Top organizational priorities WIIFM Positive impacts of the project	
Barriers	Uncertainties Negative impacts of the project	
Communication Preferences	Project communication needs Current communication methods	

Chapter 5

Daily time log

Start time	End time	Communication activity	Duration	Was this planned communication?	Comments
TOTAL TIME SPENT					

Communications management plan table of contents

Table of Contents	Suggested Content to Include:
1. Overview and Purpose	• Introduction • How to use this document, and its value • Communication strategy or approach • Consider this section as an "executive summary"
2. Organizational Policies and Procedures 　a. Communications Processes 　b. Technology and Information Storage	• Company communication policies and standards • Approval processes • Information about technology that the project team will be using • Where project information will be stored • How to retrieve project information
3. Stakeholder Communications	• Stakeholder requirements and expectations • List of key stakeholders • Do's and don'ts when communicating with stakeholders
4. Communications Matrix	• Communication requirements • See Table 5.1 in Chapter 5 for an example
5. Change Control	• How changes will be handled and communicated

6. Project Team
  a. Contact Information
  b. Roles and
      Responsibilities
  c. Reports
  d. Meetings and Calls
	• Team member names and locations
	• Contact information (e-mail, phone, etc.) including emergency contacts
	• Roles and responsibilities for each position on the team
	• List of reports, their purpose, when to use
	• Details around conducting project meetings and team calls including agendas, expectations, protocol, etc.

7. Signatures	• Signature of the project sponsor and/or executive management to show commitment and approval
8. Appendix 1: Glossary of Terms/Abbreviations	• List of important terminology and/or abbreviations
9. Appendix 2: Communication Templates	• Sample templates
10. Appendix 3: Communication Examples	• Sample communications
11. Version Control	• Revision numbers for historical reference

Chapter 7

Template for tool selection criteria and priority

Criteria	Must have	Would like to have	Do not need
1.			
2.			
3.			
4.			

Status report template

Project status report	**Status:** ☐ Green: On track (within cost, schedule, scope parameters) ☐ Yellow: In jeopardy ☐ Red: Off track
Submitted by:	
Role:	
Project name:	
Reporting period:	
Report date:	

Project objective

Project status	*Include color (green, yellow, red) and explanation*
Overall	
Scope	
Schedule	
Budget	
Other	

Tasks	*Completed since last report*

Tasks	*Working on (Progress on these tasks will be stated in next report)*

Issues/risks	*State problem, status, and next steps*

Comments	*Include any lessons learned*

Chapter 8

Stakeholder change map template

Stakeholder	What should they know about the need for this change?	How will the project impact them?	What support will they need to take the actions required for project success?	What will reinforce the change with this group, even after the project ends?

Chapter 9

Stakeholder conflict template

	Stakeholder 1	Stakeholder 2	Stakeholder 3
Stakeholder 1			
Stakeholder 2			
Stakeholder 3			

Chapter 10

Action plan template

Skill to work on	Steps to implement	Due date	Chapters to review	What does success look like?	Done √

APPENDIX D

Key Questions

For ease of reference, the key questions which appear at the end of each chapter are listed below.

Chapter 1

1. What successes and challenges have you experienced when communicating on projects?
2. How would you answer this question: If so much has been written about effective communication in projects, why does ineffective communication continue, risking project success?
3. Now that you have explored the evolution of project communication through the lens of the *PMBOK® Guide*, describe your own journey in communicating on projects. How has your approach to communicating on a project evolved over time?

Chapter 2

1. In your opinion, what are the similarities and differences between the way uncertainty is defined in communication theory and in project management? Discuss your findings with other stakeholders, colleagues, or classmates.
2. How does a stakeholder's influence affect the way you communicate with them? In your next stakeholder interaction, document your experience.
3. Select an opportunity where a stakeholder initiates communication with you. Can you discern any uncertainty that might have motivated the stakeholder to reach out to you? Is it an uncertainty you could have addressed in your project communications management plan?

Chapter 3

1. Describe your experience in communicating with stakeholders. What situations have been the most successful and/or the most challenging? What advice would you give to new project managers in communicating with stakeholders?
2. Using the five classifications of stakeholder engagement, what communication strategies would you use to move a stakeholder from a position of resisting your project to a more supportive role?
3. Working with your project team, develop stakeholder personas using the template provided. What categories or questions would you add? What value do you see in using stakeholder personas?

Chapter 4

1. Review the "Things to Consider" section at the beginning of this chapter. What would you add from your own experiences when communicating on projects?
2. In your next communication interaction or project team meeting, intentionally put the six active listening skills listed in this chapter to use.
3. Try delivering the same message in seven different ways and see the difference. Then share the results with your project team.

Chapter 5

1. Create a time log for tracking your project communications. For 1 or 2 days, track how much time you spend communicating on the project. Review the results. What surprised you? What didn't surprise you?
2. What challenges or project risks might you encounter if your project team does not have a project communications management plan?
3. Take a look at the list of techniques presented in this chapter to ensure your project communications management plan is being used effectively. What other techniques would you add to the list and why?

Chapter 6

1. In your project communications, how are you addressing the personal needs and practical needs of your project team members, sponsor, and stakeholders? Write them down.
2. Count the number of times you ask your project team members and/or stakeholders, "What do you think?" Track the results. Share with others.
3. What techniques are you using to measure the effectiveness of your project communications? List them. Note which techniques are working, and where changes are needed.

Chapter 7

1. What criteria would you put on your list when selecting a project communication tool for your project? How would you prioritize your criteria?
2. What is your project "story"? Share it with your team and colleagues or record it as a video. Get feedback from others.
3. Do you use your talents and strengths as a project communication tool? If yes, how do you use them in communicating effectively within the project team, and with other stakeholders? If no, how can you start using your talents and strengths more effectively?

Chapter 8

1. Think of the last project you worked on. How was change communicated? What change communications could have been improved?
2. Consider the four change management concepts in the "Communicating Change" section of this chapter. How would you apply them to communications in a current or recent project?
3. Have you ever experienced change fatigue? What were the factors that contributed to it? How were you able to address these factors to overcome change fatigue?

Chapter 9

1. Think back on your project experiences where conflict has occurred. Was it task conflict or interpersonal conflict? How was it handled? If it occurred again, what would you suggest be done differently?
2. When you have experienced conflict on a project team, what communication strategies have you used? What adjustments to these strategies have you made?
3. What benefits have you experienced or seen from positive conflict on a team? What challenges have you experienced or seen when conflict goes unresolved?

Chapter 10

1. Using the S.U.M. technique, write down one or two key learnings for each of the following questions: What information in this book has been most surprising for you (S)? What information has been most useful (U)? What information has been the most memorable (M)? Share your answers with a colleague, team member, student, or professor.
2. Develop your action plan for improving your project communications. What key skills would you include? To get started, list three skills you would like to improve, with at least one actionable step you can take to build each skill. Share your action plan with a colleague and ask for their help in holding you accountable for progress and completion.

APPENDIX E

Sample Ground Rules

Here is a list of sample ground rules as described in Chapter 4. This is just a sampling. Select the ground rules that fit your team. Develop and reword ground rules together. This should be a collaborative exercise—at the start of the project—with everyone on the project team. This ensures the team's buy-in, commitment, and understanding. During the life of the project, it may be necessary to add or modify some ground rules. However, strive to keep the list to a reasonable number and as static as possible, to avoid confusion. Post the ground rules in a location where everyone on the team has easy access and quick reference.

General Communications Practices

- Ask questions to learn more and gain understanding.
- Support your opinions with facts.
- Be open and honest—no hidden agendas.
- Appreciate new ideas and different perspectives.
- Define acronyms to avoid confusion.
- Frequently check for understanding—summarize and/or paraphrase.
- Do more listening and less speaking.
- Respect one another.
- Share your knowledge—and encourage others to share theirs.
- QTIP: Quit Taking It Personally.

Meetings

- Start and end meetings on time; respect those who have shown up on time.
- No backtracking for people who are late.
- Come prepared to all meetings.
- Have an agenda—publish and distribute it at least 48 hours in advance of the meeting time.
- Attend all meetings; if you are unable to attend, submit your individual status report to the project manager.
- Focus the discussion to the current topic.
- If the discussion is stalled, ask the facilitator to use the 5-minute rule (come to closure in five minutes so that the group can move on).
- Everyone is responsible for the success of the meeting.
- Be an active participant—everyone participates.
- Listen intentionally and take accurate notes.
- Avoid distractions; turn off (or silence) electronic devices.
- One conversation at a time—no side talking.
- Don't interrupt while another person is talking.
- Silence or absence means consensus.

Status Reports

- Use the designated status report template.
- Submit status reports to the project manager by (certain date and time).
- Follow the guidelines set in the project communications management plan for submissions.
- All members of the project team are expected to read all status reports.
- If a report contains important information for stakeholders, that information should be called out separately, not just buried in the report.

E-mail/Files

- Answer all team members' e-mails within (a specific number of hours).
- Answer stakeholder e-mails within the same day, if possible.
- Set specific rules around who should be copied on e-mails and when.
- Use clear, descriptive subject lines so recipients know what the e-mail is about and can easily locate it later.
- If your e-mail contains a request or assignment, provide a clear, specific deadline of when you need it.
- Keep e-mail threads on topic. If you need to discuss a new topic, start a new e-mail rather than a reply.
- Use proper file naming conventions and post files in the project information repository.

Problem Solving

- Strive to solve problems among the team.
- If a problem needs to be escalated, all involved parties meet with the project manager (or sponsor).
- When a problem occurs, the team will discuss three to four alternatives, and prepare one recommendation for the project manager (or sponsor).

About the Authors

Connie Plowman is a certified project management professional (PMP®) and an experienced chief operating officer. She puts her communication skills to use in her leadership roles—as a corporate executive, educator, volunteer, mentor, and project advocate. She is a project management instructor and guest speaker, helping to develop the skills of emerging project managers and business leaders. As a participant on diverse global project teams, Connie has experienced how effective communication can truly drive project and team success.

Jill Diffendal is a seasoned writer, editor, communicator, and adminis-trator with a passion for engaging audiences across a wide range of in-dustries through traditional, electronic, and new media. She has spent her career communicating with people around the world through both operational and project-based work, focusing on stakeholder engagement and realization of benefits. As a communication subject matter expert, she emphasizes—and has experienced first-hand—the value and benefit that effective communication brings to projects, teams, and organizations.

Index

OTHER TITLES IN OUR PORTFOLIO AND PROJECT MANAGEMENT COLLECTION

Timothy Kloppenborg, *Editor*

- *Quantitative Tools of Project Management* by David L. Olson
- *The People Project Triangle: Balancing Delivery, Business-as-Usual, and People's Welfare* by Stuart Copeland and Andy Coaton
- *How to Fail at Change Management: A Manager's Guide to the Pitfalls of Managing Change* by James Marion and John Lewis
- *Core Concepts of Project Management* by David L. Olson
- *Projects, Programs, and Portfolios in Strategic Organizational Transformation* by James Jiang and Gary Klein
- *Capital Project Management, Volume III: Evolutionary Forces* by Robert N. McGrath
- *Capital Project Management, Volume II: Capital Project Finance* by Robert N. McGrath
- *Capital Project Management, Volume I: Capital Project Strategy* by Robert N. McGrath
- *Executing Global Projects: A Practical Guide to Applying the PMBOK Framework in the Global Environment* by James Marion and Tracey Richardson
- *Project Communication from Start to Finish: The Dynamics of Organizational Success* by Geraldine E. Hynes
- *The Lost Art of Planning Projects* by Louise Worsley and Christopher Worsley
- *Project Portfolio Management, Second Edition: A Model for Improved Decision Making* by Clive N. Enoch
- *Adaptive Project Planning* by Louise Worsley and Christopher Worsley
- *Passion, Persistence, and Patience: Key Skills for Achieving Project Success* by Alfonso Bucero
- *Leveraging Business Analysis for Project Success, Second Edition* by Vicki James
- *Project Management Essentials, Second Edition* by Kathryn N. Wells and Timothy J. Kloppenborg
- *Agile Working and the Digital Workspace: Best Practices for Designing and Implementing Productivity* by John Eary
- *Project-Based Learning: How to Approach, Report, Present, and Learn from Course-Long Projects* by Harm-Jan Steenhuis and Lawrence Rowland
- *Developing Strengths-Based Project Teams* by Martha Buelt and Connie Plowman
- *Scrum for Teams: A Guide by Practical Example* by Dion Nicolaas

Announcing the Business Expert Press Digital Library

Concise e-books business students need for classroom and research

This book can also be purchased in an e-book collection by your library as

- *a one-time purchase,*
- *that is owned forever,*
- *allows for simultaneous readers,*
- *has no restrictions on printing, and*
- *can be downloaded as PDFs from within the library community.*

Our digital library collections are a great solution to beat the rising cost of textbooks. E-books can be loaded into their course management systems or onto students' e-book readers.
The **Business Expert Press** digital libraries are very affordable, with no obligation to buy in future years. For more information, please visit **www.businessexpertpress.com/librarians**.
To set up a trial in the United States, please email **sales@businessexpertpress.com**.